Praise for *The*

'In The Spiritual Password, *Princess Märtha Louise and Elisabeth Nordeng give us clear and simple guidance as to how to reconnect with our spiritual selves, the essence that we exist as in between our physical lifetimes. With elegance, ease and grace, this book shows us how to live that essence here on Earth.'*
Dr Eric Pearl, world-renowned healer and author of the international bestseller *The Reconnection*

'*The conventional approach to understanding the nature of life has focused on assessing the mechanics of the physical plane. In contrast, the new science emphasizes that life is shaped by the mechanics of the energetic or spiritual realm. In their highly readable book, Princess Märtha Louise and Elisabeth Nordeng offer valuable insight and simple practices that enable readers to move beyond misperceived limitations and create lives overflowing with love, peace and happiness.'*
Bruce H. Lipton PhD, cell biologist and bestselling author of *The Biology of Belief*

'The Spiritual Password *will empower you to reawaken your true self, reveal your inner gifts and revitalize your connection with the loving energies of the universe.'*
Taro Gold, bestselling author of Open Your Mind, Open Your Life

The SPIRITUAL PASSWORD

The SPIRITUAL PASSWORD

Learn to Unlock Your Spiritual Power

Princess Märtha Louise & Elisabeth Nordeng

HAY HOUSE

Carlsbad, California • New York City • London • Sydney
Johannesburg • Vancouver • Hong Kong • New Delhi

First published and distributed in the United Kingdom by:
Hay House UK Ltd, Astley House, 33 Notting Hill Gate, London W11 3JQ
Tel: +44 (0)20 3675 2450; Fax: +44 (0)20 3675 2451; www.hayhouse.co.uk

Published and distributed in the United States of America by:
Hay House Inc., PO Box 5100, Carlsbad, CA 92018-5100
Tel: (1) 760 431 7695 or (800) 654 5126; Fax: (1) 760 431 6948 or (800) 650 5115
www.hayhouse.com

Published and distributed in Australia by:
Hay House Australia Ltd, 18/36 Ralph St, Alexandria NSW 2015
Tel: (61) 2 9669 4299; Fax: (61) 2 9669 4144; www.hayhouse.com.au

Published and distributed in the Republic of South Africa by:
Hay House SA (Pty) Ltd, PO Box 990, Witkoppen 2068
Tel/Fax: (27) 11 467 8904; www.hayhouse.co.za

Published and distributed in India by:
Hay House Publishers India, Muskaan Complex, Plot No.3, B-2,
Vasant Kunj, New Delhi 110 070
Tel: (91) 11 4176 1620; Fax: (91) 11 4176 1630; www.hayhouse.co.in

Distributed in Canada by:
Raincoast, 9050 Shaughnessy St, Vancouver BC V6P 6E5
Tel: (1) 604 323 7100; Fax: (1) 604 323 2600

Text © Princess Märtha Louise and Elisabeth Nordeng, 2009, 2014

First published in English by iUniverse in 2012. Originally published
in Norwegian under the title: Møt din skytsengel, copyright © 2009
by CappelenDamm Forlag, Oslo, Norway.

The moral rights of the authors have been asserted.

The information given in this book should not be treated as a substitute for
professional medical advice; always consult a medical practitioner. Any use of
information in this book is at the reader's discretion and risk. Neither the authors nor
the publisher can be held responsible for any loss, claim or damage arising out of the
use, or misuse, of the suggestions made, the failure to take medical advice or for any
material on third party websites.

A catalogue record for this book is available from the British Library.

ISBN: 978-1-78180-267-0

Interior images created by Strong Design

To our greatest teachers:
Ulvar, Lea Caspara, Maud, Brage,
Maud Angelica, Leah Isadora
and Emma Tallulah

$\mathscr{C}$ONTENTS

PREFACE

We are living in extraordinary times. This is because we are going through a major energetic change. The enhanced energy flow that has now become available to us is transforming many of our lives. What was important to us in the past may look shallow and uninteresting today. We are being encouraged on many levels and in various ways to live our lives from our highest potential. Perhaps you would like to undergo this transformation too and live your life as it was meant to be, fulfilling your purpose, but do not quite know how. Maybe you have already opened up to your spiritual side but feel it is difficult to bring it into everyday life. Rediscovering your Spiritual Password may change your life, as it changed ours.

Our common spiritual journey started in 2003, when angels brought us together. Inspired by the angels, we found our Spiritual Password and rediscovered our true path as lightworkers. In 2007, we founded Astarte Education, now called Astarte Inspiration (*please visit www.astarte-inspiration. com for more details*). In addition to giving inspirational seminars, teaching workshops and releasing spiritual books around the world, we run a three-year course featuring energy readings, healing and a touch method that we have developed.

This book is based on the experience we have gained through connecting to our Spiritual Password and opening to our inner guidance, conversing with angels and teaching at Astarte Inspiration. It offers both theory and practice. The theoretical section explains the different stages of the meditations and exercises we present and illustrates them with our own and other people's personal experiences. The identity of the participants remains confidential, and everybody concerned has given their consent for their story to be included.

In the appendix we offer advice to those who are new to meditation as well as to those who have been meditating for some time. We hope it will be of assistance if you get stuck. It may also help you to listen to the meditations rather than having to learn the different steps by heart or look them up in the book, so for extra support we have recorded a CD, *The Spiritual Password: Meditations*, which is also available to download (please visit www.astarte-inspiration.com for more information). The recorded meditations may differ slightly from the written text, but the message is the same. Of course you can also get somebody to read the meditations to you.

If you have any questions regarding your experience during meditation, please contact us via Twitter (@spiritualpasswd) or Facebook (The Spiritual Password) and we will try to answer all your questions to the best of our ability. By talking about your challenges, you may help someone else struggling with the same issues – a win–win situation.

If you expect this book to satisfy your intellect, you will be disappointed. It goes without saying that you have to use your brain when it comes to understanding the theory, but the important thing is that if you choose to do the meditations, you have to allow your experiences to unfurl without your intellect interfering either during or afterwards. If you read this book with your intellect only, you'll miss what is behind the words, namely an encounter with yourself.

The most important thing we wish to pass on is the excitement and happiness of having an honest encounter with yourself. When you reconnect with yourself via your Spiritual Password, you might discover personal qualities you didn't know you possessed. Finding your Spiritual Password is easy, as easy as one, two, three, because you already know it, you've just forgotten that you know it. Through rediscovering it, you'll find a vast number of possibilities opening up for you. Do you remember what it was like to go treasure hunting as a child? Now you'll have the chance to feel the same breathless anticipation. But this time, you are the treasure.

PART ONE

The Path to the Spiritual Password

ℐNTRODUCTION

'Boundaries? I have never seen one, but I have heard
that they exist in the minds of some people.'

THOR HEYERDAHL, EXPLORER

Each and every one of us comes from light – the same light, where we are all connected, consciously, as part of the Oneness, also referred to as the Field. The experience of Oneness disappears for most of us at some point during our childhood years. The interesting part is that when it happens, we're oblivious to the fact that we've lost one of the most sacred and natural connections we possess as human beings: the true connection to the Divine. Through the shutting down of this natural contact, as well as the loss of our connection to ourselves and our surroundings, we lose an important key – the Spiritual Password, our unique connection to the wisdom of our heart.

The tricky part is that if we yearn to recover our password, our connection to our inner truth, we can't seem to recall it. We can't find the way.

This happened to us too, although we came from very different backgrounds. Princess Märtha Louise is the daughter of King Harald and Queen Sonja of Norway and has been in the public eye since birth, while Elisabeth Nordeng was brought up in an average Norwegian family. Nevertheless, while growing up we had very similar experiences of feeling different because of our spirituality. Both of us were highly sensitive people, taking in everybody else's emotional and physical tension. We saw energies around people, we could sense unspoken truths and we both had healing hands. To us, this was normal – we thought that everybody could sense the same. It hit us hard the day we realized that this was not the case.

Trying to adjust to the intellectually oriented society around us, we started closing down our sensitivity as much as possible. In this way we turned off our inner navigational systems and started forgetting our Spiritual Password. We felt disconnected, alone, different, insecure and energetically drained. Our intellect couldn't satisfy the questions that kept recurring with greater intensity throughout our youth: is there something more to life than the physical plane we all agree exists? If there is, how do we connect to it and for what purpose? Why do I sense things that others don't?

Trying to find answers to these questions, we signed up for the same clairvoyance course. There were 15 people on the course, and to be honest we didn't click with each other straight away. We didn't click at all. We can remember – with horror, we might add – the three times we tried to strike up a conversation. It wasn't until the course had ended, two and a half years later, and we were continuing to do energy readings with the group, that we had a conversation on the subject of angels and our contact with them. That was when the angels removed a veil between us and we suddenly saw that we had the same sense of humour and the same dream of working as a spiritual teacher. Going from not managing to complete a sentence to each other to finishing each other's sentences in an instant was nothing short of a miracle. We understood that we had been preparing for this moment all our lives.

It was through our collaboration that we rediscovered the Spiritual Password and instantly reconnected consciously to the Field. From being physically drained by something as normal as being around other people to being able to keep our energy levels up throughout the day, no matter what the challenges, was simply astounding to us. We intuitively understood the significance of finding the Spiritual Password and knew that it was too important to keep to ourselves.

We all have our very own Spiritual Password. Finding it takes only a minute of our time. Learning to use it takes a lifetime, but with that password we can be connected to our divine self and to the Field every second of our conscious life, and we can shine as the light we truly are.

We find that at this time there is an urgency for each and every one of us to re-enter a conscious life where we know who we truly are: a divine light. Please join us in rediscovering your Spiritual Password and reconnecting to your heart, the Earth, the source of the universe... and your guardian angel. The world needs you as a lightworker right now.

$\mathscr{T}$HE CHAKRAS

To understand how we can regain awareness of our connectedness to the Field, we need to understand the laws of nature and how to get in contact with both our physical energy (our body) and the subtle energy field surrounding us (our aura).

We are all equipped with senses that enable us to experience the physical world around us. It's easy to forget that there is more to the world than what these senses perceive. Everything in the world consists of energy. Some vibrates on such a high, fast level that we perceive it as mere energy, while some vibrates on a lower, slower level, which we perceive as physical form.

If we break matter down, we find it consists of atoms. According to mathematician and physicist Niels Bohr, atoms consist of protons and neutrons, which constitute the nucleus of the atom, and electrons, which orbit that nucleus just as planets orbit the sun in a solar system. Protons have a positive charge, neutrons no charge at all and electrons a negative charge. Atomic structures in turn create molecules, which constitute the physical world surrounding us.

According to cell biologist Bruce H. Lipton, atoms actually consist of infinitesimally small whirls of energy. From a distance, we see them as a blurry sphere. At close range, we can't see anything, since atoms have no physical structure. When scientists study the physical attributes of an atom, such as mass and weight, the atom will look and behave like physical matter. When the same atom is described in terms of its charging potential and wavelength, however, it will exhibit the properties of energy. Our building blocks are, in other words, comprised of energy that we perceive both as subtle energy and as physical substance. This was discovered by physicist Albert Einstein. He revealed that we live in one indivisible, dynamic whole, where energy and matter are so closely entwined that it is impossible to see them as independent entities.

In practice we can compare ourselves to a light bulb. The bulb itself is physical energy, but it only glows if electricity – subtle energy – flows through it. It's the same with us. Our physical body, which is denser energy and therefore can be perceived by our physical senses, can't live without the subtle energy flowing through it.

We can see that energy contributes to physical reactions, for example in the interaction between nerve impulses and muscles. Nerve impulses, in the form of electric signals from the brain, travel through the network of nerves to the muscles of the body, which then contract and movement occurs.

Apart from these specific impulses, the body is permeated with energy. This vital energy is found in all life. In India it is called *prana*, in China it is named *chi* and in Japan *reiki*. In the Western tradition, it is often described as 'spirit' or 'life-force'.

In order for this energy to communicate with the physical environment, there are special portals, or energy points, in the body. These are known as *chakras*. They are meeting points for physical, psychological and spiritual energy. Humanity has known about these chakras for thousands of years, but it is only in the past few hundred years that we in the Western world have gained detailed knowledge of them. In earlier times, chakras were not only known to people in the Orient, but also to the Native American cultures. However, the most famous descriptions of them originated in India and the yogic tradition. The word *chakra* is derived from Sanskrit, the ancient Indian language, and means 'spinning wheel' or 'wheel'. These wheels spin in different directions on men and women.

The Traditional Description of the Chakras

In the subtle energy system of the body, there are more than 360 chakras of various sizes. They are spread all over the body, including in each of our joints, in our hands, on our feet and in our inner organs. The most important have traditionally been the seven chakras that run through the centre of our body from the lower part of the pelvis along the spine and all the way up to the top of the head (crown):

* The root chakra is located below the pelvis.

* The hara chakra (or sacral chakra) is situated just below the navel.

* The solar plexus chakra is located in the soft tissue region below the sternum.

* The heart chakra is situated in the middle of the chest.

* The throat chakra is located in the throat.

* The third eye chakra is situated in the middle of the forehead.

* The crown chakra is located on the top of the head.

The chakras spin at different speeds, which is why they are described as different colours. When light is deflected through a prism and divided into colours from red to violet, the red vibrates more slowly and the violet vibrates more rapidly. The range of chakra colours is structured in the same way – like a rainbow. The chakras that spin more slowly are more closely connected to the body and the physical environment, and those that spin more quickly are more closely connected to the spiritual plane, so create our subtle energy field.

Each chakra can be linked to a different part of the physical body. An imbalance in a chakra may lead to physical discomfort, and physical strain can in turn create a chakra imbalance. We won't go into detail about which parts of the body are connected to which chakras in this book, but will list the connections between the seven main chakras, the glands of the body and the areas of life to which they relate:

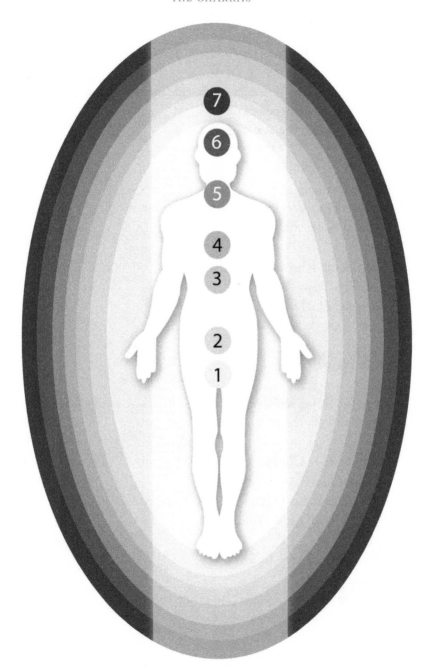

The Seven Chakras

The Root Chakra
Colour: red
Area: grounding (contact with the Earth), the ability to cover the basic needs of life
Physical glands: the sexual glands

The Hara Chakra
Colour: orange
Area: sexuality, creativity, creative power
Physical gland: the pancreas

The Solar Plexus Chakra
Colour: yellow
Area: personal power and will, fulfilment
Physical glands: the adrenals

The Heart Chakra
Colour: green
Area: self-love, self-worth, love for others, universal love
Physical gland: the thymus

The Throat Chakra
Colour: blue
Area: communication, identity, self-expression
Physical gland: the thyroid

The Third Eye Chakra
Colour: indigo
Area: sight, both physical and intuitive
Physical gland: the pineal gland

The Crown Chakra

Colour: violet
Area: the spiritual self, contact with the universe, contact with God
Physical gland: the pituitary

When we have an idea, it will enter the crown chakra and travel through all the other chakras before it is born and established as a reality from the root chakra. However, in the course of our lives, we experience misfortunes that remain in our body as trauma. This settles both in the physical body, in the form of tension, and in the energy body, in the form of imbalances or chakra blockages. So, the idea has to get through all these built-up layers of untreated physical, psychological and spiritual material, and parts of it are stopped by fear, feelings of inferiority or other illusions every time it reaches a new layer. This means that when it finally sees the light of day, it is often very different from the original thought.

You might have experienced this yourself. Maybe you've had a brilliant idea. But when reason has come into play or you've been affected by fear, you've dismissed it. Or, if you have taken it forward, you've limited it to something you believe others will understand and accept.

This is why it's so important to get in touch with these blockages and dissolve them. When energy flows freely between the chakras, all kinds of things may start to happen – both large and small. When fear disappears, you'll also dare to give your intuition a chance. By following your intuition, you may reach out to people you'd never have talked to before. Perhaps they will turn out to do the same things as you or know someone who does. Those people in turn may have contacts that make it possible to carry through your original idea. We call these sort of events 'divine coincidences'; they are miracles of everyday life. Alternatively, when you dissolve your blockages, you may make choices that lead you to a point where your original idea is brought to life. This means you can go with the flow and live in your own truth.

The Chakra Systems of the New Era

We are living in a time of energetic change on Earth. This started several years ago and will continue for some years to come. As a result of the new energy coming in, not only are our lives undergoing tremendous transformations, but our energy systems are too. The ever-increasing rapidity of the incoming energy is demanding the development of faster energy structures. If you want to make a faster car, you must replace the engine. But the new engine won't work at optimum power until the other parts of the car have been upgraded too. This also applies to our energy body.

This is why we are seeing more and more of what up to now have been called indigo and crystal children in the world today. We find that this is not an adequate term for people of the new era, though, as a lot of these children have been grown up for a long while now, and therefore we will call them indigo and crystal *people* from now on. Indigo and crystal people have always been present on Earth, but in far fewer numbers. The times are now changing, and indigo and crystal people will soon be the majority of the population, enhancing and supporting the energy shift that is already occurring. They bear the frequencies of the new era.

Indigo people are named after their indigo aura. They only have three chakras: the root and hara chakra are joined in the hara chakra; the solar plexus, heart and throat chakras are joined in the heart chakra; and the crown and the third eye chakras are joined in the third eye chakra. The areas these chakras represent, in life and in the body, are also joined.

The chakras of the indigo people have also begun working more as a unit. That is to say, they have started spinning at about the same speed. So, they don't have different colours and only differ in shade:

The Hara Chakra
Colour: pale indigo
Area: grounding (contact with the Earth), the ability to cover the basic needs of life, sexuality, creativity, creative power
Physical glands: the sexual glands and the pancreas

The Heart Chakra
Colour: medium indigo
Area: personal power and will, fulfilment, self-love, self-worth, love for others, universal love, communication, identity, self-expression
Physical glands: the adrenals, thymus and thyroid

The Third Eye Chakra
Colour: indigo
Area: sight, both physical and intuitive, the spiritual self, contact with the universe, contact with God
Physical glands: the pineal and pituitary glands

This information is new and revolutionary, and delving into it will enhance our understanding of the new times already

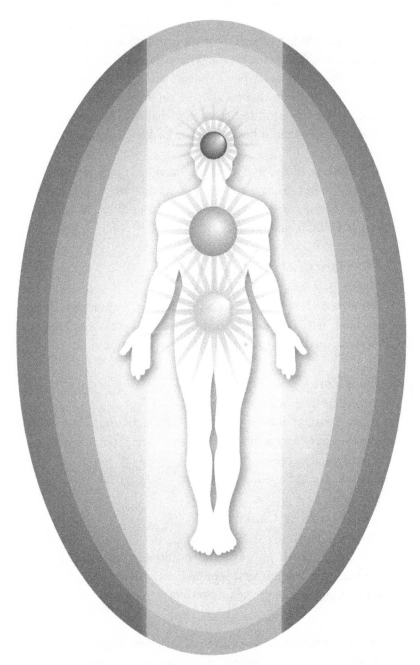

The Chakras of Indigo People

ignited. Indigo people can in fact be described as a wake-up call to previous generations. They are often conscious of the environment and fight for the survival of the Earth, emphasizing sustainability, saving threatened species, and so on. They are determined people who stand up for their rights. They are clear about what they want in life and aren't afraid of authority.

Crystal people have a different kind of energy again, resembling the energy of crystals. In crystal people, all three of the indigo people's chakras are joined in one chakra: the heart chakra. This chakra is consequently larger than the chakras of the other systems and the energy structure is changed so that bodily functions operate as a whole, in one impulse. This is partly why crystal people can manifest what they want in life very quickly.

We can compare the different chakra systems with an ordinary postal letter, an analogue connection and a broadband connection. The seven-chakra system is like a letter: after it is mailed, it goes through a lot of hands and takes time to reach its destination. The three-chakra system of the indigo people is like an analogue connection that sends, receives and downloads e-mails quickly. The crystal people's sole-chakra system is similar to a broadband connection that handles several tasks at the same time and is very fast.

So, there is a vast difference between how people with these different chakra systems manifest results in life. People with a seven-chakra system like to manifest in a straight line. That is to say, when you do A, you end up at B, and then you can start moving towards C and D, and so on. The road is mapped out, with little room for improvisation. Indigo and crystal people, on the other hand, set their goal and before

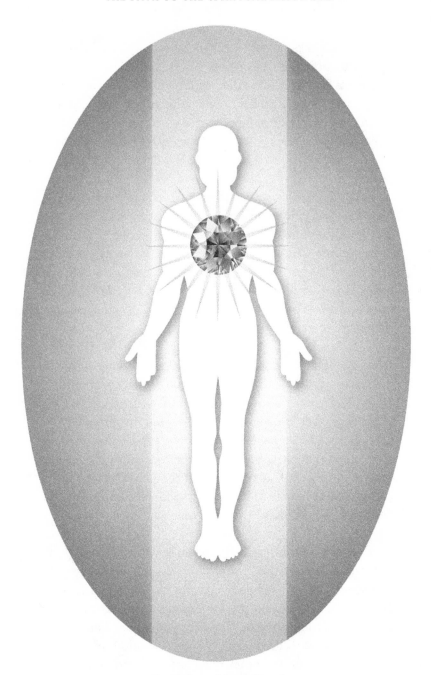

The Chakras of Crystal People

they know it, they've met someone, heard something or got the information they need from a totally unknown source and have reached their goal in the blink of an eye. How they get there is mostly based on impulse, improvisation and what others might perceive as sheer luck, but these people are closely connected to the Source. Creating through their intuition comes naturally to them. Because they have fewer chakras, they also have fewer chances of blocking what they want to create through fear and low self-esteem, and therefore they put many more of their ideas into action.

These two ways of creating are of course very different, and when people using them meet, they tend not to understand one another very well. By being aware of the difference between the chakra systems, however, we can heal this so that we can co-exist and take the best from each way of creating, while respecting our differences and knowing that although we do things differently, we are of equal value as people.

Another potential problem is that because indigo and crystal people have such strong intuition and can sense more than most people, this may frighten those around them. As a result they try to adjust by switching off their highly sensitive systems so they are more like the people in their environment.

ELISABETH:

> As long as I can remember, I've felt different. A lot clicked into place when I took my spiritual side seriously and started living it out. Still, something indefinable was missing. Even though I tried to look at the chakra systems of the people around me and imitate them, it often just intensified my loneliness and my feeling of not being in charge of my own life, even though

*I seemed fine outwardly. The root chakra and the energy
connection from there to the Earth felt heavy. It wasn't right for
me. It was a great relief when I discovered there was more than
one chakra system. For the first time in my life I felt at home
in the world and in my own body. I could vibrate within the
chakra system that was right for me.*

The fact that you have a different chakra system from the
people around you doesn't make you better or worse than
them. All chakra systems have the same value. It is, however,
important to find out how your energy is structured. Many
people who believe they have a seven-chakra system actually
don't have that system. But whether you have a one-chakra
system, a three-chakra system or a seven-chakra system is
irrelevant in the sense that we are all equal.

2

$\mathscr{T}$HE PHYSICAL BODY

Our physical body – that is to say, the energy body we call physical – is, contrary to our subtle energy field, something we all agree exists. We can, without a doubt, experience it with all our senses. But although we're totally dependent on our physical body for our existence here on Earth, we tend to lose contact with it for a variety of reasons, including tension, trauma, unhealthy food and society's focus on the intellect. It is therefore important to re-establish communication with it. We're using the word 're-establish' deliberately, since most of us communicated with our body as a child.

We might have lost contact with our body growing up, but in the course of a day we may communicate with it a lot more than we think. How do we know that we're nervous, for example? Perhaps by feeling our stomach knot or getting sweaty palms. Maybe our knees knock together. All this is information from our body. It is saying, 'This is a situation I'm not comfortable with. Let me run away from it!' To take other examples, when our body is tired, we get sleepy. When our body needs nourishment, we get hungry. There are many ways our body communicates with us.

Our Inner Compass

We are all also equipped with an inner compass, or a pilot, if you like. It can be called 'a gut feeling', 'intuition' or 'following your own star'. This compass guides us both in difficult situations and in everyday decisions, based on our own criteria and our own truth. It can manifest itself so that we simply know what is right for us, that we see one alternative shining more brightly than the other, that we hear an answer or that we feel which direction our legs should take us in.

The way we have built our society has led us to disregard these small pieces of advice from the body. There are for instance many people who suppress the hunger signals of the body with endless diets or by choosing a profession which gives them security rather than following their own dreams. But the more we disregard these bodily signals, the further we travel from our true path. When we switch off our body's signals and live as if other people's opinions are more important to us, we gradually lose our original communication with our body.

There may be lots of reasons why we stop communicating with our body. Stress can be a real factor. When we're busy achieving everything we've made up our mind to do, it's easy to lose touch with ourselves. Or the cause might be a traumatic incident in our childhood. It may be the fact that we weren't seen, we weren't loved, we were lonely, a beloved family member died, we were subjected to psychological or physical abuse, or something similar. The pain can become so strong that finally it feels too hard for us to be present in our body. Every time we are, we experience the untreated pain. The result may be that we learn how to switch off the pain. Or that we even choose to leave our body, leaving only a small part of ourselves there.

There are people who live the majority of their life with parts of themselves outside their body. Have you ever experienced suddenly seeing yourself from the outside? Or said that you were 'beside yourself' – without realizing that you actually *were* beside yourself?

When we are in this position, it becomes even more difficult to communicate with our body – partly because we don't want to feel pain, partly because when we aren't completely present in our body, we intercept the signals of our body less clearly. The first step towards re-establishing contact with our body is therefore to be aware of where we are. The following meditation may help.

(If you experience any kind of problem during meditation, or wonder how to get started, first create a quiet space for yourself then follow the steps below. The appendix at the back of this book has more tips on establishing a meditation routine. You can also download the meditations by visiting www.astarte-inspiration.com. We hope this support is of assistance to you.)

❧ MEDITATION ❧

BODY AWARENESS

Sit on a chair, close your eyes and take a few deep breaths.

Feel where you are present in your body right now. Are you present in your toes? Are you present only in the upper part of your body or only in the lower part of your body? Are you more present in the right half of your body than in the left? Are you present in your stomach?

Explore and feel for a while.

Become aware of where you are outside your body. Are you above your body? Are you below your body? Are you to the right or to the left of your body? Are you in front of or behind your body?

Thank yourself for the steps you have taken, and thank your body for what it has shown you.

When you have finished, you may open your eyes.

You may wonder whether what you experienced during your meditation was real or was just a figment of your imagination. It can be hard to tell the difference. We suggest that you trust your experience. This is *your* reality, *your* communication with your body. What if you didn't feel anything at all? Even that tells you something about yourself. And if you feel that you are only fantasizing during meditation, that tells you something about yourself too. It is all information about where you are right now. If you have any questions regarding your experiences during any of the meditations, please contact us on Twitter (@spiritualpasswd) or Facebook (The Spiritual Password).

Regaining communication with your body is like getting back into speaking a language you haven't used for a long time. You still remember quite a lot, but don't recall what everything means, so you may feel uncertain about your experiences.

In addition, next time you do the meditation, you may have a completely different experience. This is because you aren't in the same situation. You aren't starting out from the same point. No experience is right or wrong. So, no matter what you experience during meditation, just leave it at that without bringing your intellect into the equation. Without analysing.

MÄRTHA:
>One day when I felt a bit absent-minded and cut off from
>my feelings, a friend of mine asked me where I was, because,
>as she pointed out, I wasn't with her. This made me look at
>myself with new eyes and I realized that I was more or less
>floating freely outside my body. I discovered that I normally
>looked at myself from above and it struck me that whenever
>I thought I was present in my body, I was only present in my

head and chest, never in my legs. This was the beginning of my new body awareness.

In the previous meditation, you may have realized that you weren't fully present in your body either. You may have filled your body to your throat or your chest. Or maybe you were only present in one half of your body or in one of your toes. You may have experienced a line or a border that you couldn't manage to cross, a barrier that prevented you from taking up a great deal of space in yourself. This may be a defence that you've put up for yourself in order to avoid unpleasant feelings or memories, for example grief, anger, loneliness, or even something completely different, known only by you.

What's filling the rest of your body when you aren't present? Only you know that, too. It might be other people's experiences or truths that you've made your own and are living by. It might be other people's energies. By that, we mean someone else's way of thinking or experiencing the world, which is not necessarily your own: your mother's way of looking at herself as a victim, your father's strictness, your teacher's way of assessing you. It could be anything.

All kinds of trauma may settle in the body in the form of muscle tension. No doubt you've felt the level of tension increase in your body before an exam. Your neck and shoulders stiffen and you get a knot in your stomach. When the exam is over, the tension disappears too. But when it comes to trauma, the tension isn't always released. Your body may retain it in order to protect you.

As we have seen, the atoms of the body may be perceived in two ways: physical (weight and mass) and non-physical (charge and wavelength). That is to say, everything in our body is both physical and energetic. So, when our body carries trauma, it does so both through physical tension and through tension in our energy. This means we can dissolve the tension both with physical touch and through energy work, i.e. meditation, healing, energy reading, and so on. Different methods can give the same result. And behind all this lies our true potential.

MÄRTHA:

> When I was learning the Rosen Method of bodywork, I was scared to death of reaching my heart of hearts. I was convinced that deep down I was an evil person and I was scared of having my true self revealed. But one day when I dared to open the door and was face to face with myself, there was only love within my heart of hearts: love of myself and of the world that I'd been afraid to show in case it was taken away from me. So I'd conjured up the most frightening thoughts, images and feelings as a fence around it.

> Since then I've realized, through my own experiences and through meeting other people, that what we hide deep down is often what we're afraid of having taken away from us. What we hide is not how terrible we are but our greatness and our inner source of infinite love.

In the previous meditation, you got to know where you are present inside or outside your body. In this next meditation, which is about breathing out resistance to being present in your own body, remember that you may have the same experience again or a completely different one. Both are real. The only thing you have to do here is to encounter yourself. And if you feel you can't do that fully, that will also tell you something about yourself.

✿ MEDITATION ✿

BREATHING OUT RESISTANCE

Sit on a chair and close your eyes.

Take deep breaths in and out. Every time you breathe in, breathe in more of yourself and your own energy. Every time you breathe out, breathe out resistance, other people's energies or any other feelings that emerge.

Sit like that for a while, breathing in more of yourself and breathing out other people's energies. Let whatever wants to emerge come up to the surface.

Feel where you are present in your body right now.

Are you only present in the upper part of your body or only in the lower part of your body?

Perhaps you are present only in the right or the left part of the body…? Or perhaps you are present from your knees downwards.

There is often a line of resistance preventing you from going further than your chest. Are you encountering that?

Go to the division line (or one of the division lines if there are many) between where you are present in your body and where you are not.

Meet the resistance and breathe it out. Inhale more of yourself and your own energy, breathe out more

resistance and feel it giving way. (You may need to
breathe in and out a few times before it loses its grip.)

Go to the next place where you feel resistance and
breathe out what you find there. And every time you
breathe in, draw more of your own energy, more of
yourself, into your body.

Keep on breathing like this until you feel the resistance
go. It doesn't matter whether it takes two breaths or ten
minutes of breathing.

Thank yourself for the steps you have taken.

When you have finished, you may open your eyes.

Did you manage to let go of the resistance? Did it feel the
same or different in the various parts of your body? Did
you have more space for yourself in your body or not?
Remember that whatever your experience, it's valuable
information for you.

Initially when you start communicating with your body in
this way and allow yourself to feel, you might notice pain
here and there. It's as if your body's saying, 'Now that
you're finally taking notice of me, I want you to know that
I'm actually in pain here – and here too.' It's best to take it
easy when such pain emerges, to feel its presence and thank
your body for letting you know about it and work with it.

It isn't always easy to meet pain and discomfort. When
we're ill, we take medicine in order to feel better, and when

we're in pain, we often just want to ignore it. That's why we should be glad when pain manifests itself. We should try to be grateful to our body for responding to us.

When we encounter aspects of ourselves that we feel uncomfortable about, however, it can be all too easy to judge ourselves. If you experience this during meditation, just try to encounter yourself with acceptance, curiosity and happiness. Let it be like a first meeting, where you're receptive and have no preconceived ideas. And remember that your meditations won't always be the same. Just allow yourself to go on this journey with greater awareness of yourself.

The first step towards encountering yourself with love is accepting where you are right now, with all your shortcomings. So, the greatest gift you can give to yourself right now is to tell yourself that you're good enough the way you are.

$\mathscr{T}$HE AURA

'The power of life is not confined to a human, but
radiates around her like a sphere of light.'

PARACELSUS (1493–1541), SWISS DOCTOR AND FOUNDER OF
MEDICAL AND PHARMACEUTICAL CHEMISTRY

Although atoms are mere energy, they are measurable both
physically and energetically. Our body, too, perceives them as
both matter and energy. The subtle energy field surrounding
the body is called the aura.

The aura is an egg-shaped field of subtle energy that originates
in our core. Traditionally, it is described as consisting of
several layers and communicating with the body through the
chakras. There are innumerable descriptions of the aura from
the point of view of a seven-chakra system. Some people say
that it consists of the same colours as the chakras, with red,
which corresponds to the root chakra, being closest to the
body and violet, which corresponds to the crown chakra,
farthest away. According to this view, the colours of the
rainbow are therefore represented in the aura as in the seven-
chakra system, and the different layers are called bodies and
have different functions, which correspond to those of the

chakras. Some people, however, believe that these layers are structured differently and the colours don't correspond to the chakras in the same way. Yet another view is that there are only five layers in the aura, and some say that the outer part of the aura is golden.

There are fewer descriptions of the auras of indigo and crystal people. Their inner structure is simplified. As a crystal person has only one chakra, their aura consists of wholeness. The auras of indigo people are somewhere in between the one-chakra and seven-chakra systems. We choose not to give a detailed description of the structural mechanics here, as they aren't needed in rediscovering the Spiritual Password. The important thing is to know what an aura is.

Moving the Aura's Edge: One of the Best-Kept Secrets of our Time

Our aura stretches from 30–50 centimetres (1–1½ feet) outside our body when it functions optimally – about as far as our wrist if we hold our arm out straight ahead of us. The edge of the aura – the egg-shaped silhouette – can be seen as the boundary between us and other people. It is like a cell membrane and protects us from the unwanted energies of other people. It is semi-permeable – that is to say, it lets through certain energies but not all.

In Indian and yoga traditions, there are 72,000 energy channels, called *nadis*, in our subtle energy field. They connect the aura and the chakras with our physical body. They are also called *meridians* and are the energy system used in acupuncture. They can be compared with the circulation of the blood, as they provide cells with the vital life-force, just as the blood vessels provide the cells with nutrients.

The aura works as a halfway station for everything we take in and everything we release. For example, energies that we daren't let go of completely may be stored there. This can lead to an imbalance of the aura that after a while manifests as ill health.

We have now come to one of the best-kept secrets of our time. The function of the aura has been well-known for thousands of years, but the fact that we can move the edge of our aura consciously and that this affects our well-being is a different matter. We are very often unaware of where the edge of our aura is, but we move it unconsciously all the time and this can have a real effect on us. Do you often get energetically drained in the presence of others? This could be because of your aura. Do you get nervous or feel you would like to disappear when others are invading your space? This can be due to your aura too. Do you find that you get a kick out of performing on stage and can't sleep for hours afterwards? That could also be down to your aura. All these and many other reactions can be the result of where the edge of your aura is placed. It is therefore of vital importance to gain some knowledge and control of it.

Some people keep their aura close to their body, while others let it expand a long way out. Those who keep it quite far out – up to several metres – may find it encompasses a lot of other people. This often happens with someone who is responsible for other people or who takes responsibility for others. Someone who runs a company, for example, may take their employees under their wing. They expand their aura to encompass all their co-workers, for security, and maybe for some control too. Actors and artists often expand their aura so it embraces the whole audience. Teachers – both those teaching in ordinary schools and spiritual teachers – can expand their aura so that it encircles their students, while therapists who work one to one with clients might expand their aura so that it covers their client.

It can feel safe and comfortable to be encompassed by somebody else's aura, but it can also be limiting. When we are in this situation we tend to draw on the other person's information and energy, so we don't have to take responsibility for who we truly are and be honest to ourselves about where we are in life. It helps us to avoid taking action to live as our true selves in the world – for some reason, we are all afraid of doing just that. Therefore, we have a tendency to use other people's energy as support instead of using it as inspiration to find the same power within ourselves, ignited by the strength we value in others. It is often a comfortable and, above all, safe experience to be in the aura of a person you look up to, but it can also become trying and tiring. In a way it's like being a teenager who wants to become independent but whose parents don't want to let go.

Those keeping other people within their aura can get a real kick out of it. Actors and artists, for example, are often exhilarated after a performance. They may experience it as a substantial injection of energy. In fact they've taken energy from the people they've encompassed in their aura. Afterwards, though, they usually become very tired and energetically drained, since they've been carrying all those people's energy without being aware of it.

One reason for expanding the circumference of the aura is for protection. Some people can, for example, send their aura into a room to check out the atmosphere there, preparing themselves for what they are to meet when they walk in. Or they can 'touch' others with their aura. That is to say, they can take in other people's energies and moods and get an overview of who may be on their side and who may be against them.

But most of all we experience our aura as a boundary between ourselves and others.

MÄRTHA:

All my life I've been in the public eye, which resulted in my aura unconsciously widening as protection. For a long period, I felt that my duties as a princess were overwhelming. Since I felt that I wasn't good enough for the role, I tried to make myself popular by giving a little piece of myself to everybody I met, everybody I was supposed to meet and everybody I might perhaps meet in the future. The result was that I tried to cover the whole of Norway with my aura.

From an early age, I felt frustrated because so many people crossed the boundary to my personal space. I felt the media took more than I wanted to give, plundering my personal life. It felt as though people I didn't know were taking parts of me without asking, and I didn't like people staring at me. Finally I could barely say hello to people without my stomach knotting.

One day I did an exercise with a friend. She placed herself on the opposite side of the room and told me to imagine that I was at an official function. Slowly she began to walk towards me. I was supposed to tell her when I felt she was too close for comfort. When she was about 3 metres (10 feet) from me, I told her to stop. She laughed and said, 'How d'you think anyone is going to be able to strike up a conversation with you without trespassing? They can't even reach your hand to say hello.'

We did the exercise over and over and I had to imagine that I was in different situations: in my princess role meeting people, in private company, in town, going for a walk in the forest, at home alone and in the stables. I was surprised to see that my boundaries moved depending on how I looked upon the different environments. When I imagined that I was in the stables, my friend couldn't make me feel uncomfortable, no matter how close she got. It made an indelible impression on me. When I was in a situation where I felt safe, nobody could invade my boundaries.

Later, I realized that it was my aura that had moved in accordance with the situation I had imagined I was in. When I learned to let my aura expand to 30–50 centimetres (1–1½ feet) from my body, its natural place, the feeling of being devoured by others completely disappeared.

Every time I feel insecure, or somebody crosses the boundary to my private space for no apparent reason, I check my aura. In nine out of ten cases, it has expanded too far.

You might think that Märtha's different reactions had to do with her comfort zone, meaning the distance from other people, for example during a conversation, in addition to what she was comfortable doing in her life. But the comfort zone and the position of the aura are two different things. The comfort zone varies from person to person. It is a psychological border between what we are comfortable with and what we are not in all areas of our life: work, personal and professional relations, living quarters and what we share with others. The Dalai Lama says, 'Life begins at the end of the comfort zone.' Elisabeth experienced just that through her spiritual path:

ELISABETH:
In the past I was a very shy person and doubted my mystical experiences, so what I wanted from the clairvoyant course where I met Märtha was to meditate under an apple tree. That was within my comfort zone at the time. The course emphasized energy readings, which are a soul-to-soul communication. Therefore my comfort zone expanded to sitting under my apple tree and giving readings to other people, one at a time.

When we started Astarte Inspiration in 2007, my comfort zone expanded yet again, to teaching 25 students at a time. But by consciously giving to myself and actively 'clicking' my aura into place (both of which you will learn later on), I still had the experience of sitting under my apple tree.

The next step was to challenge myself to a far greater extent. Märtha and I were scheduled to give our first inspirational talk together at an alternative expo. We assumed there would be approximately 150 people in the audience, maybe 200 if we were lucky, and were shocked to learn that there would be 1,000 people there. It was a huge step for me, but once I was in the situation, it was extremely inspiring and a lot of fun. Since then Märtha and I have appeared on large TV shows and given workshops all over the world, and I can think of nothing more worthwhile. And it still seems to me that I am sitting and meditating under my apple tree.

Sometimes I wonder where I would be today if I had stayed in my comfort zone and not listened to my heart and to the angels guiding me.

Expanding our comfort zone means increasing our possibilities in life and not being held back by our fears and limitations. We can expand our comfort zone by making sure our aura is in its optimal position. Then we're able to be aware of who we are in every situation. People can cross our boundaries and we can still be consciously present in our space. We will look at how we can click our aura into place later on.

Even though we may not be aware of where our aura ends, we can still affect others through it. We can even push them with it. This may be most clearly seen when we're out hiking, skiing or walking up a steep hill.

ELISABETH:
> When I was in my twenties, there was a steep path from the bus stop to my home. One day when I was quite tired on my way home from work, I was dawdling at my own pace along the path. Behind me there was a man who apparently viewed the road as a workout opportunity. Long before he got close to me, I started to walk faster and faster. In the end I had to surrender, step aside and let him pass.

That is how we use the aura for communication without words. You may remember a childhood hike when your mother or father said, 'You first, so you can set the pace.' But even if you were first, your parents may have thought you were walking too slowly. So you might have walked faster and faster, without anybody saying anything. When we're out walking, it's easy to notice such aura pushes', but they happen all the time when meeting others. When somebody pushes our aura, in any situation, it's easy to slip away from our own pace and let others set it.

We have explored the effects of keeping the edge of the aura far away from the body, but there are also many people who have a different protection strategy, i.e. keeping their aura close to their body. This may be the result of some kind of violation of their boundaries. Those who keep their aura tight to their body are trying to hide from the world around them, to melt into the background, to make themselves invisible.

ELISABETH:
Because I used to be so shy, especially when many people were present, I often got nervous and found it difficult to come out with the right words – that is, if I dared say anything at all. As I got to know more about my own aura, I discovered that when I was among a lot of people, I kept it close to my body. I was trying to protect myself, to make myself invisible. But instead it made me feel naked and skinless.

Now that I'm in touch with my aura, I know how to keep it where it works best for me. When I encounter other people, I can feel protected and secure about myself.

It might sound a little too simple to say that if you change the position of your aura, everything will be fine. Obviously, changing the position of the aura doesn't solve everything, but it can make a substantial difference. When the edge of the aura is optimally placed in relation to the body, it works as a natural defence against other people. When it is too far from us or too close to us, we take in other people's feelings, pain and energy along with our own. It becomes difficult to feel where we end and others begin.

When children first learn to paint, they mix all the colours unconsciously, the result being a murky colour that no one but their mothers can say is beautiful. Later, when they develop a conscious approach to the colour palette, they mix the colours beautifully and create wonderful pictures. This is what happens to our energies too. When we unconsciously mix with other people, holding our auras too close or too far away, we become unclear, not knowing who's who or what's what. When we're conscious of where we place the edge of our aura, however, we can mix energies, be inspired by and exchange information with others and still be crystal-clear about who we truly are.

How do we know that we have found the right position for the outer edge of our aura? The wisdom of our body re-enters in this situation, because the body shows through various signals when the edge of the aura is in its most favourable position. One of these signals may be a clicking sound when it reaches that position. That's why we call having the aura in its optimal position 'clicking' the aura into place.

There are many different ways of experiencing the aura clicking into place. People who see the edge of the aura might see a certain colour or shadow; other people may feel cold or warm. Some may even smell a distinct odour or get a specific taste. Others simply know.

Perhaps you're wondering how to get in touch with your aura. It's not as difficult as you might think. In fact, you're probably moving it around unconsciously all day long. With the following exercise, you can begin to find out how to move it at will.

✧ EXERCISE I ✧

MOVING THE AURA

Stand straight with your arms along your sides and close your eyes (or keep them open if you want to). Take a few deep breaths.

Let your body show you where you are currently holding the edge of your aura. Is it far away from you or close to you?

Pull the edge of the aura to you, or push it out, depending on where it is situated, so it moves to where it should be, about an arm's length from you. To do this, it might be helpful to imagine yourself inside a balloon. To pull your aura closer to you, simply let the air out of the balloon so that the sides draw closer. To push your aura out, simply fill the balloon with air and let the sides expand.

Feel, hear or see your aura clicking into place.

Reach out with your hands to check that it is where you think it is. How does it feel to have it there? Take some time to listen to what your body tells you.

Now move the edge of your aura outwards until it is 1 metre (around 3 feet) from you and push it slowly farther out until it is about 3 metres (nearly 10 feet) away.

Feel what it is like to have it so far away from you. Does it feel familiar or unfamiliar? In what situations do you keep it away from yourself?

Moving your aura

Push it even farther out to experience how it feels. Do you experience any physical reactions when it is that far out?

When you are ready, let the edge of your aura move back to where it clicks into place and then pull it back slowly until it is about 1 centimetre (½ inch) from your body.

Feel what it is like having it so close. Does it feel familiar or unfamiliar? In what situations do you keep it so close, if you do it at all? Does having the aura close to you create any physical reactions?

Let your aura slide back into its natural position and click into place.

Breathe out and let go of what you've just experienced.

When you start moving your aura, you may get physical reactions. This is totally normal and shows how your aura affects you daily. Many people who are used to expanding their aura find it difficult to draw it close to their body. If you are one of them and you do manage it, you might feel cramped when it is only an arm's length from your body. You might feel that you can't breathe, or that you are naked or unsafe. You might get a headache, feel dizzy, find it hard to stay present in your body or even feel nauseous. The same thing often happens if you're used to holding your aura tight to your body. When you move it out, you might feel dizzy or unsafe, get a headache or feel as though you are losing yourself.

If you're thinking *I can't manage this at all* or *What I'm feeling can't be what they mean*, then do the exercise again. Trust your feelings. There's no right or wrong here. Meeting the aura is like a child examining a flower for the first time. The child doesn't ask if the fragrance of the flower is right or the colour is correct. So, trust your senses. You have them, even if you haven't used them for a while. This is your experience of your aura, and everything about it tells you something about yourself. Listen without judgement and try to understand what your body is saying to you.

If your aura edge has clicked into place at arm's length, your own feelings and energies will become clearer. That is why it's easier to listen to yourself and your body when your aura is in place. When you know who you are and where your boundaries lie, it will help other people to see who you are too. So your aura will become a defence, preventing unwanted energies from entering your space. As a result, you'll find it easier to keep up your energy levels, since you won't have to give energy to everybody within your aura at any given moment.

When you keep the edge of your aura a long way away from yourself, you're like a draughty old house with heat leaking out – more energy is necessary to keep it as warm as a well-insulated house. When the aura edge is in the right position as regards your body, you consume less energy in the course of the day since your energy is no longer going to other people but to yourself. This in turn will give you more strength.

ELISABETH:

> When I first started learning about energy work, I met a
> woman who told me I had several holes in my aura. Aura
> holes are like blind spots where other people's energies can enter
> unnoticed. Consequently, my boundaries were blurry to myself,
> as well as to the people around me. Often I felt some kind of
> indefinable anxiety. Did it belong to me or to other people?
> Wherever it came from, the result was a strong feeling that
> something wasn't right. This in turn made me leave my body.
> Only there could I feel protected.
>
> Through meditation and energy work, I found my outer aura
> edge ended up where it worked best for me and clicked into
> place. It gave me new awareness of myself and my boundaries.
> It gave me inner peace and security when I met other people.

The next exercise will help you to explore your aura further,
this time with your hands. Make sure that you click your aura
into place before you try touching it, though. Having it too
far away from you will prevent you from reaching the edge.
Placing it too close will also be confusing, although it will be
possible to touch it then, since it will be within reach.

To increase the sensitivity of your hands, rub your palms
against each other as if they are cold and you want to warm
them. This will help you to perceive the contact with your
aura more easily. If you lose touch with your aura during
the exercise, rub your palms against each other again. You
can also do it more often than we have suggested here. Feel
your way.

Don't worry if you don't get the hang of this exercise at
once. You may have to try it several times. Have patience
with yourself and listen to your body and what it tells you.

❧ EXERCISE 2 ❧

FEELING THE AURA

Stand up and rub your palms against each other fast so they get warm.

Imagine that the edge of your aura is situated about an arm's length from you and experience how it clicks into place.

Put your arms out in front of you with your palms turned at a 90-degree angle towards you.

Pull your hands slowly towards you until you reach your aura.

You may perceive your aura as hot, cold, a prickling sensation in your fingers or some resistance; you might see a certain colour or just know deep down when you touch it with your hands.

Explore your aura with your hands in different places around your body. Focus on having it click into place.

How does your aura feel around your thighs, shins and feet? How does it feel above your head? Is there a place where it bulges in or out, or where it seems to be missing?

You are now going to move the back of your aura and place it in front of you. Rub your palms against each other again, turn your palms outwards and let them get hold of the inside of your aura, as though you were touching the inside of a balloon.

Explore your aura with your hands in different places around your body.

By moving your hands horizontally, rotate your aura so that the back ends up in front of you.

Explore the back. How does it feel above your thighs, calves and feet? How does it feel above your head?

Does the back feel different from the front? Is it closer or farther away from your body? Are there any holes or places where you can't feel your aura?

Rotate your aura again: take hold of the inside of the aura, with your palms facing outwards, and move your hands horizontally so that the aura rotates until the front of it is placed in front of you again.

Thank your body for the information, thank your aura and thank yourself for the steps you have taken.

Breathe out and let go of what you've just experienced.

As mentioned earlier, it can be hard to find the edge of the aura; it might be too far away from you or too close to you. You may want to do the exercise several times before you continue.

What did you discover? Perhaps you felt that your aura stuck to your body somewhere. The aura is like a surround-sound system enveloping the body, but often we forget to pay attention to the aura under our feet or behind our back, and in places we aren't aware of, it tends to stick to our body. Accordingly, its function is minimal there. When we observe the position of the aura edge and can put it in place, however, the aura ceases to stick to our body. Simply feeling where the aura sticks to the body, or noticing a hole, is often enough for the aura to adjust itself. As long as we are aware of a certain situation, the energetic body can heal itself in the most miraculous ways. The key seems to be awareness, because if we are unconscious of a situation, we can't do anything about it. We don't even know it exists. But the second we are consciously aware of a situation regarding our aura, it will instantly start the healing process.

The next step is to feel somebody else's aura. Find a friend you trust and who would like to do this exercise with you. It may be fun for both of you.

✆ EXERCISE 3 ✆

FEELING SOMEONE ELSE'S AURA

Stand on opposite sides of a room, facing each other. One of you is going to move the edge of their aura and the other will feel where it is with their hands. Decide who is going to do what before you start. Let us call the person moving their aura A and the person searching for the aura B.

A lets the edge of their aura click into place at arm's length from their body.

B rubs their palms against each other till they are warm and starts walking forwards with their palms turned towards A.

B stops where they feel the edge of A's aura and then returns to the starting point.

Still standing in the same place, A then moves the edge of their aura 2–3 metres (6½–10 feet) away.

Feeling someone else's aura: A (right) pulls in the aura to just a few centimeters from the body. B (left) stops where they feel the edge.

B again rubs their palms against each other till they
are warm and starts walking forwards with their palms
turned towards A.

B stops where they feel the edge of A's aura and then
returns to the starting point.

A pulls in their aura to just a few centimetres from
their body.

B rubs their palms against each other till they are warm
and starts waking forwards with their palms turned
towards A.

B stops where they feel the edge of A's aura and then
returns to the starting point.

A then moves their aura in or out, without telling B
where it is.

B is now going to find out whether A is keeping their
aura tight to the body, a long way out or clicked into
place. (Of course, it is important that A keeps their aura
in the same position until B can feel it.)

Run through the process a few more times in different
positions. Then change over and do the exercise all
over again.

Did it surprise you that it was so easy? Maybe you thought
that it would be possible to feel the aura when you knew
where it was. Feeling it when you *didn't* know where it was
may have been slightly surprising. This exercise shows that
a person can move the edge of their aura consciously and
that other people can feel that aura.

With this new awareness, you can now go out into the world and feel where your aura is in different situations. It certainly made a difference to Lucy.

> *Lucy was an airline stewardess, and her workday consisted of meeting lots of people in the confined space of an aircraft. As she was highly intuitive, she would take in extensive information from everybody and often end up totally drained after a day's work. When she learned to click her aura into place at one of our workshops, her life started changing. Meeting people no longer drained her and she could keep her space during the day. She thought that working in such a tight space as an aeroplane was great aura-clicking training!*

Taking your aura seriously is important for your wellbeing. Remember, your aura is as much part of your body as your physical energy body. Play with it and explore. See how other people react when you suddenly let it expand a long way or pull it in really tight, but most important of all, see how you feel when it has clicked into place just where you should keep it in relation to your body – and how it affects you.

Awareness of where you place your aura is life-changing, so try to be conscious of where your aura is placed in your everyday life. This might sound like a big task, but it only takes a bit of training. Start the day by clicking your aura into place and notice where you keep it during key moments such as when you're in your car, at work and grocery shopping. Whenever you feel invaded, or energetically drained, check your aura and see whether it is in place or not. It only takes a second to click it back and it makes such a difference.

The most important thing is awareness and then the healing process can start.

4

$\mathcal{T}$HE SPIRITUAL PASSWORD

Now that you've begun to communicate with your body and aura, you can also begin to communicate with your heart. This is part of the Spiritual Password, but before we reveal the secret of this password, we will explore the physical heart. As the physical and energetic parts of the body are pure energy in different forms, they are equal in value and it is just as important to get in contact with both of them.

The Physical Heart

The heart is the meeting point between Heaven and the Earth – between the spiritual and the physical world. It is the meeting place for the universal love within and around us. It is from this point that we give love to ourselves and others and receive love in return.

The heart is placed in the centre of the body. Since it pumps the blood, it is the source of life reaching all parts of the body, both physically, with the blood, and energetically, with the heart chakra distributing energy through the meridians. When the blood is pumped by the heart and flows at a steady pace, we can experience our heartbeat everywhere in our body as a pulse. Tension and blockages can prevent us from hearing our heartbeat in the same way everywhere in our body, however. This tells us something about our situation right now. But in a second it can be different. We are constantly changing, developing and growing. What we are dissatisfied with today, we can change tomorrow.

It is important, however, that we accept ourselves the way we are. So, consider everything you encounter in the next meditation as loving information for yourself. And remember that all information is of equal value.

❧ MEDITATION ❧

FEELING THE HEARTBEAT IN YOUR BODY

Sit on a chair, close your eyes and take a few deep breaths.

Let the edge of your aura click into place at arm's length from your body.

Feel where you are present in your body right now.

Put one of your palms, or both, on your heart.

Be aware of your heartbeat against your palm.

Start listening to your heartbeat. Do you hear it or do you feel it? Or do you neither hear nor feel it? Do you experience a colour or a tone? Or do you simply know that the communication is there? Remember that everything has the same value and whatever you feel just tells you something about yourself right now.

Breathe out any resistance – any people you meet or feelings that emerge. Breathe in more of yourself and your own energy.

Now move your attention to your throat. Are you aware of your heartbeat there?

Breathe out any resistance – any people you meet or feelings that emerge. Breathe in more of yourself and your own energy.

Move your attention to your head. Are you aware of your heartbeat there? Once more, use your breathing to get in touch with the area.

Now move your awareness to your stomach. Are you aware of your heartbeat there? Use your breathing again.

Go through your whole body in the same way, breathing out tension and resistance in every place. Take your time and pay attention to the information you receive. Breathe in even more of your own energy. Be aware of your heartbeat in your pelvis, shoulders, upper arms, forearms, hands, fingers, seat, thighs, knees, legs, feet, toes and back.

Focus on your heart again. Do you experience it in a different way now or is it the same? Both results have the same value – they are just information.

Thank yourself for the steps you've taken, and thank your heart for the information it has given you.

When you have finished, you may open your eyes.

Many of us have, in the course of our life, only felt our heart when we've experienced fear. When we're scared and our heart is beating quickly, we tend to pay attention to it. In the same way, we listen to our body when we experience ill-health or pain. So it's only when danger threatens that we take the time to listen to our heart and be considerate to ourselves. It's as if there is some programmed blockage to easy and loving communication with our heart.

Take a minute of your time now to encounter the blockage and breathe it out.

In which places did you feel your heart most clearly? In which places did you feel it least clearly? Maybe there were a few places where you didn't feel it at all.

All this is information about yourself. So, accept it, and try to accept yourself and simply observe what's happening now. This is a way of getting to know yourself again. You may have used a major part of your life to criticize yourself. Our inner judge is very often quick to judge ourselves. It is deeply programmed in many of us to be severe on ourselves. Now you have the chance to approach yourself in a new manner: with love.

It is easy to underestimate the experiences we get when connecting to our heartbeat. Some people can feel their heartbeat pulsating in their head as a loud pounding. But what if all you experience is a pale blue light? You might disregard it because it isn't what you think you're supposed to experience, but you're experiencing it all the same. So, explore it. Be curious about it. Is the colour the same throughout your body or does it change? Perhaps your heart talks to you through colours. Why disregard it? Try to be curious, whatever emerges, even if it's a black wall. A black wall – what's that doing there?

What if you're one of those people who doesn't feel their heartbeat at all? Some people are surprised to find they don't hear or feel their heartbeat. They're astonished that they haven't noticed its absence. They find out that they've taken the centre of their own existence, their heart, entirely for granted. This awareness is a fantastic gift and from now on the heart can finally begin to speak its true language, namely the language of love.

YOU SHALL BE TRUE

You shall be true.

But not to any man who in cold greed clings to your hands.

Not to any ideal flashing in big letters but not touching your heart.

Not to any commandment making you a stranger in your own body.

Not to any dream you haven't dreamt yourself...

When were you true?

Were you true when you knelt in the shadow of other people's false gods?

Were you true when your actions stifled the sound of your own heartbeat?

Were you true when you did not deceive the one you did not love?

Were you true when your cowardice put on a disguise and called itself conscience?

No.

But when whatever touched you made a tune.

When your pulse gave rhythm to your movement.

When you were one with what sparkled inside of you.

Then — you were true.

ANDRÉ BJERKE (1918–85)

The Tone

A tone, a sound wave, is a frequency. What a specific tone can achieve can seem like magic. You may have heard that singers can break crystal glass using only their voice. If the singer hits the exact frequency of the atoms of the glass, they will absorb the sound waves and vibrate more quickly. Eventually they will vibrate so quickly that they will break free of the bonds that keep them together. When that happens, the glass will shatter. So, a tone, which is energy, contributes to breaking glass, which is physical, into smithereens, because it is energy too.

Sound works in a similar way on the physical structures of the body and on the energetic blockages and tension held in the body. Therefore we can use tones to dissolve the tension, blockages, resistance, fear and so on that have settled in our body. In the next meditation, we will use our own voice.

It may feel slightly unfamiliar at first to sing a tone out loud when totally alone in a room, and even stranger to do it with other people. A lot of people are afraid of letting their voice be heard by others. Don't let it discourage you.

ELISABETH:

I am rather unmusical and tone deaf, and the first time I did this exercise I was really afraid of other people hearing my voice. I was dreading it in fact and almost felt sorry for the man sitting next to me. How it sounded to the others occupied my mind most of all. But after a while I got into my body and met my own sound and resonance and let them manifest, and they were beautiful, which was a tremendous relief. I could sit down together with other people with my own sound.

There is strong and deep healing when we allow sound to work in us. Now I know that my sound is beautiful.

❧ MEDITATION ❧

LETTING GO THROUGH TONES

Sit on a chair, close your eyes and take a few deep breaths.

Let the edge of your aura click into place at arm's length from your body.

Feel where in your body you are present right now.

Put one of your palms, or both, on your heart and feel your heartbeat. Experience it in your unique way. Feel it in your stomach, in your legs, in your arms, in your back, in your shoulders, in your chest, in your throat and in your head.

Become aware of any places where you don't feel your heartbeat and where you feel resistance. Choose one of these places.

You are going to find a tone for this resistance. Just sing whatever tone enters your consciousness. There's no right or wrong here. Sing the first tone that comes to you. Whether it's deep and thick or high and clear, welcome it and sing it out. Singing quietly doesn't help much, so go for it at the top of your voice. You may as well do it more than once.

Now find the note that will dissolve this tension and sing that out. Repeat it a couple of times. Feel how it is vibrating in your body.

Let go of everything that emerges and breathe in more of your own energy, your own essence. Feel what happens.

Find the tone of your frequency in this part of your body. Sing it out. Let the tone vibrate throughout your body. Feel how your body responds.

Repeat these three tones – the tone of the resistance, the tone that dissolves the resistance and the tone of your frequency – in various parts of your body. Take your time.

Pay attention to your heart again. Become aware of the heartbeat in your chest. Has anything changed or not?

Thank yourself for the steps you've taken. Thank your heart. Thank your body for being co-operative.

When you have finished, you may open your eyes.

Did the resistance have various tones in the different parts of your body or not? Were the tones of the resistance, the dissolving of the resistance and your own frequency different from each other or not? Did they vary in the different parts of your body? Did you feel how the tension and resistance disappeared? How is your body feeling now? Are you feeling lighter or heavier in your body? Again, all this is useful information for you.

This exercise with tones is excellent if you're stressed out. You can meet the stress where it is centred in your body, find the tone to dissolve it and find the tone of your own frequency to calm yourself down.

There are unlimited ways of using the tones. Be curious and listen to what your body's telling you.

Remember to listen to your physical heart from time to time. It might tell you something new every time. Having an honest communication with your body and your physical heart opens you up to the possibility of being present in every moment of your life. This in turn means experiencing your life to the full. The only thing missing now is the Spiritual Password.

On the Track of the Spiritual Password

When we are born, we already know the Spiritual Password, because it's natural to have contact with our inner essence. It's therefore very easy for us to get hold of the Spiritual Password, even today. In fact, we most likely knew it not only as a baby but also as a child. We simply forgot it, not recognizing its importance. It is common, as we grow up, to learn to listen to other people more than to ourselves. Maybe we've turned down the volume of our inner voice and directed our antenna towards the world and become uncritical of what channel we put our 'radio' on. Or we may have forgotten to increase the volume of our inner voice, or even forgotten that we have one. But if we don't listen to our own voice, we're living in accordance with other people's truths and not our own.

To get back to living according to our inner voice, we need to set a few things straight. The best way to start is to separate other people's wishes for us from our real wishes. Often others have prevented us from fully being ourselves. As children, we adjust to the world around us, no matter what.

But we may have experienced not being seen or not being loved and so now, as adults, we hold ourselves back and don't take our rightful place in the world. However, the present is different from the past and we now have the chance to occupy as much space as we wish. We can take charge of our life right now. We don't need to be a victim of our past any longer. The first step is to move out the energies of other people we have unconsciously carried in our heart.

We may think that it's bad to let go of people of whom we are fond. It can seem like that every now and then. But as long as we hold on to other people's energies, we're keeping them in a certain pattern in relation to ourselves. This pattern is repeated every time we meet and it hinders both of us in moving forward, taking our next steps in life.

Carrying people in our heart might start on a very positive note. When we're in love, we open our heart to another person. This results in a great flow of love from heart to heart. But as soon as we start loving someone, the fear of losing that very special someone sets in, resulting in moving that very person into our heart to be sure that they won't leave us. So we exit the trust and flow of love and enter the control zone. And we often gather more and more people in our heart in this way.

Another reason for keeping people in our heart starts at a very early age – even before we're born. As we come into our body for the first time as a foetus, and throughout our early years, we may be surrounded by people who have closed their hearts in fear. When our hearts are open, filled with the divine light, but meet this closeness in our surroundings, it makes us distrust what we believe in our heart of hearts. We move away from our divine connection and into fear and the closing of our heart. The Spiritual Password is lost or forgotten and we not only disconnect from our heart but also lose the communication between the subtle energy field and the body. Then, since we've forgotten that the divine spark of God is in our heart, we compensate by putting people there instead. This is a poor substitute for the Divine within, and in our disconnectedness we feel even more alone. However, when our subtle energy field and our body start interacting once more, the divine light will come through again and we won't need to hold on to anyone because we'll trust that we're lovable.

Another reason for holding on to people in our heart could be that we believe that we're helping people by keeping them there. We may believe that they can't take care of themselves, that they have too heavy a burden to carry, and we therefore take the responsibility ourselves, knowing we have the capacity to do so – we who can tackle anything! It is possible that we can help someone in this way for a period of time, but then they can't go their own way. It's like carrying a child: when they're ready to walk, if we don't put them down, they won't learn to take those first steps. They won't learn to walk, to run, to see how far their legs will take them. So it's better to put the child down and be there to help them up again when they fall. It's the same with anyone in our life. This isn't being hard-hearted. We can be there for people, a shoulder to cry on, no problem. But then we should put them back on their feet to follow their own path, not ours.

By releasing the people we're holding in our heart, we're returning the energies we're carrying to the rightful owners. There might be a positive change for all of us. For our energy isn't right for others, and the energies of others aren't right for us.

How to do it? Try the following meditation.

❈ **MEDITATION** ❈

RELEASING OTHER PEOPLE'S ENERGIES FROM YOUR HEART

Sit on a chair, close your eyes and take a few deep breaths.

Let your aura click into place at arm's length from your body.

Become aware of where you are in your body right now.

Put one of your palms, or both, on your heart.

Be aware of your heartbeat against the palm of your hand.

Inside your heart, there is a room. It may be indoors or outdoors. Enter the room of your heart and see if there is anybody else there.

Know that they are there because you have unconsciously invited them in to learn a certain lesson. You can now choose to let them go by asking them to leave through the door, one by one.

Thank each of them for what they have shown you by being there and then let them walk out the door with ease and with love for them and for yourself.

If there is someone who doesn't want to leave:

Find a tone for the frequency with which this person is connected to your heart. Find a tone for letting go of this person.

See, or feel, or know that this person is letting go and walking out of the door.

Breathe out resistance, feelings and any other thing that emerges from your unconscious and breathe in more of yourself and your essence.

Find a tone for the frequency in your heart.

Keep breathing out resistance and breathing in your own essence.

Continue to let people leave until you are all alone in the room.

Look around the room. How does it feel to be alone there?

Make the room just the way you would like it to be. Let it have the shape, the windows, the size, the materials, the colours and the décor you wish.

Experience the room once more. Enjoy it!

Leave the room of your heart and be present in your whole body again. Become aware of where you are present in your body this very moment.

Feel the heartbeat in your chest. Thank your heart for what it has shown you. Thank your heart for the steps you've taken.

When you have finished, you may open your eyes.

Were you surprised to see how many people were in your heart? Was there almost no room for you? Or did you come into a big empty room? Some people feel great relief at owning the room of their heart again, while others feel empty when they find themselves alone there. This may be the result of valuing themselves for being there for others, or maybe hiding a feeling of loneliness through having many people in their heart.

The most unexpected people might be stuck in the room of your heart. If there is somebody who won't leave, do the exercise over again, perhaps over the course of a few days, until everybody has left. If you do it that way, your unconscious will keep on working on it for a while. Meantime, you may safely go on to the next exercises, whether you have made everybody leave or not. Be patient with yourself. When you do let them go, your relations to others might change.

Lene's daughter was afraid of being away from her. She'd never managed to spend the night at a friend's house and Lene always had to go and pick her up in the evenings because she only felt safe at home. Now she was eight years old, it was beginning to become a problem.

Lene did the meditation and moved her daughter away from her heart. Soon afterwards, her daughter spent the night at a friend's place. This was the first time she had dared to be away from home for a night. And that wasn't all – now she was confident away from her mother as well.

Nobody understood what had happened – apart from Lene.

Working with yourself in this way can have a great effect on those around you. This shows that what we do, what we think and the level at which we vibrate, consciously and unconsciously, have an effect on ourselves and others. When we vibrate at a certain frequency, we attract situations and people that match that frequency, but when that frequency changes in ourselves, we attract changes too. Märtha had this experience when she painted her house.

MÄRTHA:

> Our summer place is situated on a hill by the sea and is well known, since it has been in the Norwegian royal family for generations. Through this time, it has been known as the yellow house – because of its yellow colour – and the island on which it is situated is nicknamed the Yellow Island because of it. Some people, both on the mainland and on the island itself, have even been inspired to paint their houses yellow too. When I looked over to the mainland, the yellow houses matching ours would stand out to me.

> One year my husband and I had some renovation work done on the building and when the painters asked us what colour we would like the house to be, it suddenly struck us that it was possible to paint it a different colour. We ended up painting it white, changing a long tradition.

> The reactions were intense. Some people loved the new colour, especially those who already lived in white houses; they said that the house looked grander and really benefited from the change. Some were indifferent to the colour, while others were furious and even phoned the local council and asked whether we were allowed to paint that particular house white, since it was royal property. Many of these people lived in yellow houses and wanted the tradition to go on. The council had to calm things down by stating publicly that my husband and I were allowed to paint the house whatever colour we liked and that

they had never thought of the colour white as offensive, as it was a common colour along the coast of Norway.

Looking over to the mainland, I had the sudden realization that I now noticed the white houses on the shore – not the yellow ones anymore.

When the house was painted yellow, it vibrated on the wavelength of the colour yellow, which has a specific speed, and therefore it resonated with the other yellow houses in the vicinity. Naturally, when its colour changed to white, its colour wavelength and speed changed too. Again, it resonated with the houses that were painted the same colour: this time with the white houses.

When we release people from our heart, we too change vibration, just as if we were painting our house a different colour. We vibrate at a new level, taking new decisions, resonating with new people and situations and dealing with daily life in a new way. The reactions to this are usually as intense as the ones Märtha experienced when she painted her house. Some people will think the new steps we're taking are wonderful and that it's time we finally saw our own worth. These people are often those who have themselves taken these steps, or who would dare to do so. Other people will be indifferent and not even seem to notice that we've changed. Yet others will react by rejecting us, getting angry with us or trying to hold us back and keep us from changing. These people aren't mean or vindictive, they're simply happy with the way things are and seeing us change is unsettling to them. They have no desire to make any changes themselves, because that would challenge their sense of security. Instead of taking the same steps and expanding, they've decided to stay put – and it's important to respect that too.

When we make a change in our life, it's good to allow both ourselves and the people around us to have a reaction to what is going on. Whatever the reaction, it's a passing phase. If we make room for the new, while remaining steadfast and true to ourselves, we offer the same chance to others. We can't change others, but we can change ourselves, and the way we react when encountering others.

5

$\mathcal{D}$ISCOVERING THE SPIRITUAL PASSWORD

Connecting to the Energetic Heart

When you find your Spiritual Password, you find the code to your inner language, a code that reconnects you to the true essence in your heart. Everybody communicates with themselves, their body and their heart in different ways. We are the only one to know what our own particular code is. Therefore, there is no right or wrong, no one way of connecting, only our own way, and we are the only one who can rediscover it.

We will find the code by using our senses, both on the physical plane and on the energetic plane, and speaking the language of the heart. You might have been reminded of that language in the previous exercises in this book, because we have, in fact, given away the code to the Spiritual Password already.

So, how does it work? Think of a computer. Almost everyone has a computer these days. A computer needs a modem to access the internet, and the modem needs a password to do its job. It is the same with us: we all need the Spiritual Password to connect to our heart (i.e. the modem) so that our heart can do its job and connect us to the spiritual web, the Field. If the password is missing, if we can't connect to our heart, we experience a disconnection from the Oneness of which we are all part, resulting in a feeling of loneliness and a belief that we are all alone in the world. The way we rediscover the Spiritual Password, and thus the connection to our heart, is through our 'double senses'.

Just as our physical senses perceive the physical world through sight, hearing, touch, smell and taste, so our double senses perceive the higher energy levels, those that aren't understood as physical but energetic. The double senses still have the same qualities of sight, hearing, touch, smell and taste, but on a different level. If someone reads us a story, we automatically see the main characters and their environment. We might hear the drumming of a horse's hooves or the crackling of a fire. We might feel the wind against our face or the chill of ice bathing in the midst of winter. We might smell the wonderful scent of flowers or let our taste buds be tickled by descriptions of luxurious food being presented before a king. We are using our double senses right there.

The phrase 'double senses' literally comes from the fact that we use all our senses both on the physical plane and on the energetic plane: we use our eyes to see, but we have inner sight as well. We use our inner sight, for example, when we remember a sunny holiday or retell an event or a story. We may listen to the sound of a car passing in the street and we can also hear it if we imagine the same experience. We can feel when somebody is touching us or we can feel it just by imagining it. Memories may enable us to smell our grandmother's buns or even taste them.

Most people teaching clairvoyance are very focused on the visual sense, and we can use our inner sight to see everything almost in a physical way. But how limited the world would be if we only saw it and cut off hearing, touch, smell and taste. Elisabeth had this experience at the clairvoyance course we took:

> When I learned to do readings, I didn't see pictures. All the other students saw pictures or even a film running in front of them. I felt miserable about not being able to see these pictures, and not being able to share my wisdom with the person I was supposed to give a reading to. The teacher said, 'If you just work a little bit harder and try a little bit more... if you just open up your third eye more and release what is preventing it from seeing, then you'll see pictures too.' For a year and a half, I thought there was something wrong with me. My self-esteem was below zero and I nearly gave up. I was still trying to see pictures in vain. Then one day something happened. While I was doing a reading – or trying to do one – a voice came into my head, saying, 'Follow what you know. Say what you hear.' When I started talking, a lot of highly relevant information came through. I still didn't see pictures, but I'd discovered my true language, which was hearing and knowing: the auditory and kinaesthetic ways of the Spiritual Password.

All the ways of perceiving information are equally good. The important part is that we receive whatever our heart tells us in whatever form. For instance, if our heart sends us a feeling of peace and we're looking for something visual, we'll lose out on the communication. Or if we hear a whisper but overlook it because we're waiting for a tingling sensation, well, the moment is gone.

If you don't feel you're connecting to your heart, don't despair. Your heart wants to communicate with you. It is, in fact, natural for it to do so. Keep in mind that it might be a long time since you used the Spiritual Password to connect with your heart and therefore you might have lost touch with it. Have patience with yourself. You might like to try the following meditation.

If you're a visual individual, images are likely to be most prominent during this meditation. If you're auditory, you'll hear words or different tones. If you're kinaesthetic, maybe feelings will surface. Remember, everything is of equal value. Be focused on receiving, regardless of the form in which the Spiritual Password comes to you.

❧ MEDITATION ❧

FINDING THE SPIRITUAL PASSWORD
TO YOUR HEART

Sit down on a chair, close your eyes and take a few deep breaths.

Let your aura click into place at arm's length from your body.

Become aware of where in your body you are present right now.

Put one of your palms, or both, on your heart and get in touch with your heartbeat.

Begin to communicate with your heart. Remember that whatever emerges and however you may be answered, it is of value.

Ask how your heart is this very moment. Accept the answer whether you see it, hear it, know it, feel it, smell it or taste it.

Ask your heart if there is anything it wants to tell you right now. Again, be open to anything that might come. No response is too small or insignificant.

Ask your heart if there is a special place where you can reach it best.

Ask your heart if there is a specific time of the day when it is optimal to communicate with it.

Ask it anything you want.

Thank your heart for having re-established its communication with you.

Thank yourself for the steps you've taken.

When you have finished, you may open your eyes.

Congratulations! You have now consciously rediscovered the Spiritual Password, your unique way to communicate with your heart – your inner wisdom. With this password, you can literally contact anything in the universe.

Some people get a sense of love or peace when they contact their heart. Some get a sense of relief; their heart says that it was about time it happened. Some get the answers to their questions even before they ask, while others don't get a response at all, or get a black colour. If you didn't get any response, or didn't feel anything during your meditation, you may have been trying too hard and therefore haven't been open to the simplicity of the answer, or to letting it emerge. Perhaps trauma is hindering the communication. Maybe you daren't encounter what you believe is there. As we mentioned before, this is also useful information. Try to be honest with yourself about what's really stopping you. If strong feelings emerge, such as anger or grief, let them manifest.

When Susanna was doing this exercise, she couldn't stop crying. She hadn't cried since her mother had passed away when she was a teenager, and that had been 30 years before. Her father had never allowed the family to mourn their mother, and Susanna had kept her grief inside all these years. When she had finally cried it out, she felt many pounds lighter and it seemed that at last she had the freedom to live her own life.

While some people don't get in touch with their heart straight away, you might have found it easier than you expected – perhaps unnervingly so. It's often the case that when we re-experience something that once was natural to us it feels as if we're just imagining things. Or we may have learned that if we want something in life, we have to fight for it, and our heart's messages seem to come too easily, so we disregard them. If you're one of these people, know that there is a different way of living where you can create your life with ease, through love for yourself.

The more you use the Spiritual Password, the more you will understand your heart and dare to have honest contact with it. This may result in you starting to live your life according to what serves you and walking your spiritual path. Some people are afraid that listening to their truth will make them change their lives entirely and therefore shut it out, because they aren't ready for it. This is of course a choice, but since there is fear there, it might be interesting, if you find yourself in this position, to ask your heart to show you when the fear of being your true self came into your life and what triggered it. Your heart will never force you to do anything you aren't ready for, because it responds from the divine spark of unconditional love.

MÄRTHA:

When I started incorporating the Spiritual Password into my life and actively listening to my heart, it changed my life considerably. From being a full-time equestrian at international level, I became a spiritual teacher and author. The steps I was asked to take were always within what I could manage, although the change was considerable.

I now know that when I dare to listen to what my heart tells me, I will always walk my spiritual path, be safe and have immense fun... and just enough challenges along the way.

The Spiritual Password is like a language we might not consciously have used for a long time. Using it daily helps us get to the heart of it, and our vocabulary may widen. At first we might get just a slight feeling of peace, for example, when contacting our heart, but when we've used the Spiritual Password for a while, it might widen to include a certain colour, or maybe an additional message in words or through knowing. The meditation to find the Spiritual Password to the heart only takes a few minutes and can be a great start to the day.

The next step is to move from only listening to our heart in meditation to being open to listening to it in everyday life. This is a process that is different for every person. Usually when we discover the Spiritual Password, it becomes easier to recognize the messages of the heart in everyday life too, though in the beginning, they can be hard to perceive. A feeling, for example, will often be vague, and we won't recognize it for what it is, because we've ignored impulses like this for many years. But if, from now on, every time we get this little nudge we react to it, our heart will know that we've started to pay attention and will gradually strengthen the connection. So, the next time we're in a similar situation, the feeling might be stronger, or we may recognize it more quickly or trust it more.

A good exercise that helps us to get into the habit of listening to our heart is waking up every morning and thanking our heart for its communication. These words may help you to enhance your connection:

Dear heart of hearts,

Thank you for your communication with me.

I am open to listening to you in whatever form you may communicate, whether it is through feeling, seeing, hearing, smelling, knowing or tasting. I know communication with you puts me back on my spiritual path and I thank you for it.

I am safe and dare to be open to my inner light and let it shine in the world, and I know you can help me with this.

Through this connection with the heart, the Spiritual Password can assist us in every aspect of life, from the large decisions, like what direction to take, to the smaller details of everyday life, such as what our body would like for dinner tonight. Use it and ask your heart. Get used to listening to your heart when you have a break during the day, when you're in the shower or when you're doing your everyday chores. It only takes a moment.

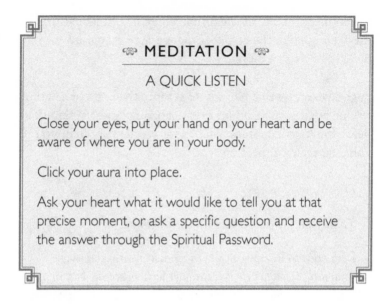

❀ MEDITATION ❀

A QUICK LISTEN

Close your eyes, put your hand on your heart and be aware of where you are in your body.

Click your aura into place.

Ask your heart what it would like to tell you at that precise moment, or ask a specific question and receive the answer through the Spiritual Password.

When you do this often, you'll be able to connect without closing your eyes and simply stay in listening mode throughout the day.

Listening to your heart will put you into loving mode. It will help you start creating your life from love and attract even more love into your life through both giving and receiving love. Once you've made the connection, you can use the Spiritual Password at will. The password may differ, as a computer connection does with different modems, but simply pay attention and you'll be able to find the Spiritual Password straight away.

PART TWO

Making Connections Through the Spiritual Password

$\mathcal{I}$NTRODUCTION

Knowing the Spiritual Password, you can now make whatever connections you like and enter whatever area of the universe may interest you. Just like surfing the internet, you simply enter the name of the web page you would like, click Enter, and, *voilà*, the page appears. If the page is locked, you then need to enter your e-mail address and the password.

It is from the essence in your heart that you connect to the Field – the spiritual web that connects us all. So, you simply need to contact your heart and choose the particular area of the Field you would like to connect to and you will make contact with that specific area. You then need to be alert for the Spiritual Password for that area so you can enter.

Would you like to try it now?

$\mathcal{T}$HE SOURCE OF
THE HEART

The first domain to delve into is the source of the heart. Physically and energetically, the heart itself may be described as a source. The physical heart, from which blood is pumped around the body, may be seen as a life-giving spring. In the energetic heart, there is an inexhaustible spring of our own energy that can spread throughout our body and nourish it.

In terms of giving, both to ourselves and others, it is important to see what the heart does physically. Since the blood supply from the main artery to the heart is located next to the heart, the heart gives blood to itself before it pumps blood around the body. If it doesn't receive a supply of blood through this circulation, this leads to cardiac arrest. We understand it so well when it comes to blood, but we don't think that the same thing applies when giving our time and attention to other people. If we uncritically give our energy without giving to ourselves, we can end up completely depleted.

The energy of the heart gives nutrients to the cells. That is why it's important to give to ourselves constantly, both physically and energetically. Just as the cells of our physical body don't work without a steady supply of blood, so our energetic body doesn't work fully without a supply of energy.

You may say, 'But if I give to myself, how can I then give to others?' Since each of us has a body with a heart, each of us has an inexhaustible source of energy available to us. It is possible for us all to use this spring in the same way that we automatically use our blood vessels to support ourselves. We don't take from others by giving to ourselves. All of us can draw energy from our spring. Therefore, it is important to get to know it – to contact the source of our heart.

❀ MEDITATION ❀

CONTACTING THE SOURCE OF YOUR HEART

Sit on a chair, close your eyes and take a few deep breaths.

Let your aura click into place at arm's length from your body.

Become aware of where you are present in your body right now.

Breathe out resistance and breathe in more of yourself and your own energy.

Put one of your palms, or both, on your heart and feel your heartbeat.

Focus on your heart. Is there anything your heart wants to tell you this very moment?

Inside the heart there is a source. You may perceive it as a lagoon, a cave, a flame or a tone, or you may just know deep down that it is there. Experience it in your unique way and know it is good for you.

Enter your heart and encounter your source. No matter how you experience it, know that what you get is of value. If you meet someone you know, let them leave, either by exhaling or singing them out.

Sit beside the source for a while, breathing out feelings, thoughts and anything else that may emerge and breathing in yourself and your energy. Feel the energy in your source. Does it have a colour? Is there a special sound there? Is there a special smell there?

Bathe in the source. Immerse yourself completely and let it envelop you.

Be aware that this is you.

Let each of your cells be filled by this source, knowing that it is inexhaustible. You can go to it at any time to be filled with new energy. There is always more. There is an inexhaustible and abundant supply.

Stay in the spring for a while and experience what it does to you.

Begin to leave the source.

Focus on the heartbeat in your chest and become aware of where you are in your body.

Thank yourself for the steps you've taken, and thank your heart and your body for what they have shown you.

When you have finished, you may open your eyes.

What did your source look like? Did it have a sound or a smell? Some people experience their source as if it is fresh, life-giving water flowing from the ground. Others perceive it as fire. Some experience it as a crystal cave, others as a stretch of smooth water next to a waterfall, or as a lagoon. Yet others may experience it as a tone or a colour or a sensation. There are as many sources as there are people experiencing them. This shows that everybody has their own Spiritual Password, their own inner language to communicate with themselves. It also means that we shouldn't compare ourselves with others in this area. Everybody is different. The only one to experience the vastness and the possibilities of the spiritual web in your very own way is you.

7

$\mathcal{T}$HE EARTH

The Earth is what gives us the experience of being human. It gives us the possibility of entering the physical plane; it gives us nutrition and the opportunity for our soul to grow through our experiences here. In addition to having contact with our body, our aura and our heart, it's important for us to have contact with the Earth. Many people seeking a spiritual path tend to disregard the physical aspect of life and set the energetic part on a pedestal. They forget that we've all chosen to be incarnated on the Earth right now, so it is of vital importance to be in contact with it through grounding ourselves. Grounding, or getting in contact with Mother Earth, is the next domain we are entering on the spiritual web.

The grounding exercises – the spiritual tools – we share with you in this chapter are innovative and revolutionary. They are techniques of the new era. We all want to keep up to date with everything, and it is important to be up to date with this. In modern times, we have all distanced ourselves from nature. We live in big cities, where tower blocks and asphalt dominate the scene. In Norway, most of us are lucky enough to live relatively close to the countryside, but in many parts of the world we have to travel a long way to get out into the countryside. There are some benefits to modern life, of course. Life was a challenge when our ancestors had to break their backs toiling. Still, they were in daily contact with nature, their animals and the cycle of the year. Since the Industrial Revolution, we have developed more efficient techniques, but replaced a lot of the close proximity to animals and other people with machines. Instead of getting together for a chat, we communicate with our friends and colleagues by means of text messages, e-mail, Facebook and the like. When we do go to the countryside, we immerse ourselves in activities like snowboarding, river rafting or racing boats and distance ourselves from simple contact with the Earth. If ever we do encounter peace and quiet, it feels strange, even boring. We get restless and busy ourselves with even more activities.

Our quest for efficiency has also affected our relationship to nature. When we are out hiking, we have to reach the highest mountaintop in order to get the best experience possible in one day.

An action-filled day out in nature can be inspiring, and it is important to play, but it is also important to be able to experience nature on its own terms, and to experience that perspective. Many people seek the peace and simplicity of nature, and a quiet walk in the woods can be one of the best things in life. It is vital to have a balance, so we can have action-filled experiences if we wish, but also wind down and take the time to get in touch with nature and the Earth – and with ourselves along the way.

Grounding

We humans are a part of nature in the same way as animals, trees and oceans. By listening to our heart, we also open up to communication with the Earth. Having open communication with the Earth from our heart is what we call *grounding*. When we have this dialogue, it makes us secure and creates an inner presence in our body and a connection with the Earth. Physically, the centre of the Earth consists of molten lava, yet through our double senses we can meet another core – the heart of the Earth – via meditation.

Environmental consciousness is growing worldwide. We buy organic food, we reduce carbon dioxide emissions to the best of our ability, we work out, we eat healthy food, we participate in the global warming debate, we use water-saving showerheads and low-energy light bulbs. All this is good. But in addition, there is a different and more profound way to go.

Just as we've learned to disregard the signals from our body, so we've also ignored our natural communication with the Earth. This is why we so often aren't grounded. Indications of little or no grounding include vulnerability, fear, stress, mood swings and restlessly moving from project to project (or from one house to another). To put it simply, we can stand less and less when we aren't present in our body and have lost our connection to the Earth.

If we're on a boat and there's a storm, we'll stand with our legs apart to weather the big waves. When we're grounded, the same thing happens: we stand steady, whatever storm may blow up. We grow strong. We get a presence in life that feels safe. We face whatever life offers. When we're secure, we're less vulnerable. So we can say that grounding gives us protection.

ELISABETH:

We have a mountain lodge and being there grounds me. Before I became aware of how important it was to be grounded, I often felt that I had to go to the mountains. Since then, I've realized that when I feel like that, I'm searching for grounding — for the lodge with no electricity and no water laid on. It is peaceful there. It is back to basics: fetching water, chopping wood and baking bread. Things we take for granted at home are things we have to work for in the lodge. I feel inner richness when the evening comes on and we have water and firewood stored inside. Being in touch with nature grounds me, and allows me to find myself. I have nothing to hide behind — I have to encounter my true self.

Of course we don't need to be in the mountains to ground ourselves. But it's easier to do so when we're in a place where we can focus on ourselves with few distractions. Once we understand how it feels to be grounded, we can establish that contact anywhere — in the city or in the country, running for the bus or at work.

Grounding enables us to be fully present in our body. It helps us to enter the present moment. It is as valuable as spiritual growth. Without it, spiritual growth can only take place on the energetic level — that is to say, outside the body — and not in physical reality.

Anne had a difficult childhood. She was often lonely and felt misunderstood by her parents and the people around her. She didn't feel seen and was left on her own a lot. As a child, she couldn't break with her parents. That's why she got angry with the Earth instead. Feeling she wanted to disappear, she began to long for 'home', wherever that was. The result was that she became ungrounded and left her own body. It was only when

*she was disconnected from the Earth that she believed she
could tackle the world around her. But by grounding herself
again, she learned to live her life from a new perspective:
present in her body and in life.*

How do we ground ourselves and get in touch with the
Earth again? First, it is important to change the view that
spiritual development is more important than daily activities.
The way we see it, they are equal.

In the book *Divine Magic* by Doreen Virtue, there are
descriptions of laws several thousand years old which were
also outlined in *The Kybalion*, a book of Hermetic philosophy
published in 1908. These are laws that the universe is said
to follow. One example is the law of attraction, which *The
Kybalion* calls the law of cause and effect, and another is the law
of correspondence: 'As above, so below; as below, so above.'
According to this law, everything happening in the higher
spheres is also happening in the lower spheres, and what is
happening in the lower spheres is also happening in the higher
spheres. This means that the same energy and spiritual growth
found in the higher spheres is found in the lower spheres, that is
to say, on the physical level. The same light, the same greatness,
exists both above and below. Just as we are overwhelmed by
the greatness of the universe, so we are overwhelmed by the
complexity of the cellular level – yes, even the atomic level.
Infinity exists both in macrocosm and microcosm.

Remember that everything is energy, even the physical
world, and therefore everything is of equal value. If we
glorify spiritual experiences, that is to say, everything
beyond our usual experience, and feel that it is only through
these experiences that we are alive, we miss out on the
spiritual growth we can have in everyday life. Secondly,

we can bring spiritual reality into everyday life. How about picking up the children from the nursery or school while totally present? Or having a meal and feeling how the food affects your body? How about going for a hike, feeling how the wind affects you? What the trees give you? How the earth feels against your feet? How about going for a hike out of gratitude for the world around you? Maybe nature will even communicate with you.

MÄRTHA:

A couple of years ago, I was in South Africa on a retreat to get in deeper touch with myself and the Earth. The leader of the course told us that elands – deer the size of cows and normally very shy – always approached the house after a healing session.

One afternoon when we were doing healing, I was wondering if these animals would appear. Unfortunately, there wasn't an eland in sight. 'That's just typical,' I muttered to myself, walking back to the house where I was staying feeling quite sorry for myself. 'They always show up when others do healings.' I was wrapped in my own thoughts when suddenly I heard a twig snap to the left. Startled, I was ready to fight a lion or whatever was about to pounce at me from the bush. But nothing came charging at me. Instead an eland was standing there, only a few metres away from me, not the least frightened. We stood there for a long time, looking at each other.

Traditional grounding extends from the root chakra down to the centre of the Earth. However, a lot of people are discovering these days that this form of grounding no longer serves them the same way, the reason being the shift in energy and our new energy structures. The three- and one-chakra systems don't have an active root chakra and therefore can't ground from it successfully. So, grounding for these new times no longer runs from the root chakra, but from the heart.

The heart is the key to contacting everything; it is also the only chakra present in all three chakra systems. People who have been meditating a lot and grounding from their root chakra find this new technique revolutionary. Even if you aren't experienced in meditation, you'll find this exercise is easy. Anybody can do it because it is natural for the body to do so. Also, by using this new grounding technique and through similar energy work, we can shift from a seven-chakra system to a three-chakra system and from a three-chakra system to a one-chakra system. What in former days might have taken a whole lifetime to achieve spiritually is easily within our reach today. That is what the new times are doing to us. They are shifting our energies so we can perceive everything around us energetically as well as physically. We are coming back to being who we truly are, in contact with the All.

Grounding from the heart is like having a communication pillar from our heart to the heart of the Earth. Through this pillar we can let go of everything we no longer need and everything that isn't ours: old memories, other people's ways of seeing our life, old thought patterns we no longer wish to follow. We can let all of this go down into the Earth. The Earth is like a big revitalizer. The heart of the Earth transforms so-called negative energies into something new and life-giving. Just as the Earth breaks down waste on the surface and transforms it into soil where new plants can grow, so it breaks down our waste energies and turns them into something new in which we can grow, such as love, security and support in life.

✿ MEDITATION ✿

FINDING THE SPIRITUAL PASSWORD TO
THE HEART OF THE EARTH

Sit down on a chair, close your eyes and take a few deep breaths.

Let your aura click into place at arm's length from your body.

Become aware of where you are present in your body.

Put one of your palms, or both, on your heart and focus on your heartbeat.

Ask if there is anything your heart would like to tell you right now.

Wait for the answer.

Breathe out any resistance, other people and feelings you encounter, and inhale more of yourself and your energy.

Focus on your heart again and feel your heartbeat against your palm.

Send a heartbeat to the heart of the Earth. Let it travel through your stomach and pelvis, down to the floor, through the floor, through the other floors if any, all the way through the ground, through the layers in the soil and right into the heart of the Earth, the centre of the Earth. Breathe out the old visions of the core of the Earth as a red-hot sphere. Allow yourself to have a unique encounter with the heart of the Earth, just as you had a unique encounter with the source of your heart.

Find the Spiritual Password to the heart of the Earth: see the heart of the Earth, or feel the heart of the Earth, or experience it as a tone, a colour or in some other unique way.

Focus on your heart again. Let a new heartbeat go completely into the heart of the Earth without following it down.

Be consciously present in your heart and start being aware of the response from the Earth in your heart. It may be a heartbeat that comes back, or a sensation of warmth, coldness, a tone, a feeling or a colour. You might just know that the communication is established. Receive the Spiritual Password with acceptance and love for yourself.

Sit for a while, with each heartbeat continuing to be an exchange of energy and communication to and from the heart of the Earth. This exchange of energies will create your communication with the Earth, your own grounding channel. Feel how it affects your heart when your energy and the Earth's energy merge there.

The heart of the Earth is a revitalizer. It transforms what we want to discard into life-giving energy. Ask your heart if there is anything it wants to let go of right now.

Let what you want to discard light up as a colour, sound as a tone, appear as an image, come to mind as an incident or be expressed in another way.

Take it into your heart in the same natural way as you drop a stone to the ground. Now let it go and let it continue down through the grounding channel.

Breathe out at the same time as you let go, and then breathe in more of yourself and your energy.

Let go of the feelings, resistance, tones, colours – yes, everything you have encountered during meditation – and send them down into the grounding channel.

Thank yourself for the steps you've taken, and thank your heart, your body and the Earth for the communication.

When you have finished, you may open your eyes.

Remember that no matter what you experienced, it is information to you about yourself. There is no right or wrong. You don't have to think *Did I do it the right way this time?*, because you did. Maybe you didn't experience anything, or maybe you didn't manage to completely reach the heart of the Earth, or maybe you had a great experience. No matter what, your experience says something about your relationship to grounding right now. It might change the next time you try. If you only covered part of the way to the centre of the Earth, you can do this meditation several times, until you finally reach the very heart of the Earth.

Humans differ so much that it's hard to generalize about the things that provide grounding. Riding and spending time at stables can ground people who like horses. But for people who are really scared of horses, just the thought of a horse may lead to a panic attack. Some people become grounded through climbing high mountains, while others are afraid of heights. Everybody, however, has a good chance of becoming grounded through relaxing, being out in nature and eating healthy food regularly.

ELISABETH:
> *I've seen how being out in nature affects my four children. At home there are many distractions in the form of television, computers and leisure activities. That is why it is pure magic to me to see what happens to the children when we go to our mountain lodge. There, away from these distractions, simply through being out in the countryside they come into contact with their body in a completely different way. It shows in their games, in how they are able to connect in new ways in spite of the age difference. They radiate a quite different harmony in themselves.*

It is important to become aware of what grounds you. Is there a special place? Is there something special you can do? Communicate with your heart about this.

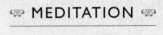

❧ MEDITATION ❧

GROUNDING

Sit on a chair, close your eyes and take a few deep breaths.

Let your aura click into place at arm's length from your body.

Become aware of where you are in your body right now.

Take some deep breaths, breathing out any resistance and breathing in yourself and your energy.

Place one of your palms, or both, on your heart. Ask your heart if there is anything it wants to tell you this very moment.

Wait for the answer and receive it, no matter what emerges.

Send a heartbeat down to the heart of the Earth and wait for the answer.

Be open to the answer, regardless of how it comes to you.

Focus on your heart and send another heartbeat to the heart of the Earth. Wait for the answer from the Earth. It may be an image, a tone, a feeling, or an idea. Accept it.

Every time you send a heartbeat to the heart of the Earth, there will be an answer.

Let your awareness remain in your heart and feel how it affects your heart to let these two energies mingle there – your own energy and the energy of the Earth.

Ask your heart if there is anything special you can do to become well grounded.

Be present in yourself and let whatever emerges be the answer.

Ask if there is a special place that gives you good grounding.

Let everything you have experienced go down the grounding channel. Let go of it.

Thank your heart for the information, and thank yourself for the steps you've taken.

When you have finished, you may open your eyes.

If you wish, you can do this meditation every now and then. What grounds you today can differ from what you'll need in a month's time. It is therefore good to take a reality check from time to time. If the same answer emerges, you'll know that you're on the right track and you can thank yourself for giving your body the best possibility of becoming grounded. If something new turns up, you can be grateful for the sensitivity to perceive it. No matter what, the answer will be positive and a gift for yourself.

Your Unique Connection with the Earth

In certain areas in life, we live on other people's energies. Growing up, it's impossible to avoid being affected by the people around us. Let's say you're a child who loves climbing trees. Your mother, on the other hand, may be afraid you'll fall and hurt yourself. She may wring her hands and cry, 'Careful! You might fall and break your leg. It's dangerous to climb like that! This is killing me! I daren't look!' In the end you too might get scared of climbing trees. Every time you do it, you may hear your mother's words or see her with your inner sight. You may experience this consciously or unconsciously. The result may be that you stop climbing trees and even become afraid of climbing altogether. You didn't start out being afraid, but you learned to be that way and to limit your physical exploration. It isn't really your fear, it's your mother's, but you've absorbed it and now you're letting it limit your choices in life.

This often happens with things we don't believe we possess ourselves or that we don't believe we're allowed to do. It is also the case with grounding. As a child, if you find that your mother gives you security and support you don't believe you yourself possess, then you might start being grounded through her. You may also be grounded through your family's grounding.

Tom was an artist. In addition, he was heir to a company. So, he studied the subjects required in order to contribute to the company, then worked for the company for a couple of years and put his art on hold.

Everything seemed fine on the surface – he had a wife, children, a house, a car and enough money – but his frustration grew. He felt that he was compromising on too many levels. The work was both stressful and hectic. Still, the thought of leaving the family business was frightening. He was afraid of not fulfilling other people's hopes for him, afraid of disappointing people at the company, afraid that he would be seen as selfish. These fears prevented him from taking the plunge.

Only when he resigned and resumed painting did his life fall into place.

This man was grounded through his family business, not through his own frequency. Even though his life seemed fine, it wasn't right for him. It wasn't until he cut off his family's grounding and had his own back that he could develop in his own life.

The opposite can happen too: if we support others, their grounding channel will go through ours. Some people even demand this. If your father, for example, claims (even unconsciously) that everything safe and good in your life – the food on the table, the house you live in, and so on – is there thanks to him and he regards the space around you – your space – as his, then you might give up the ownership of your grounding and let your father have it instead. Often we don't notice that somebody has invaded in this way, maybe because it happened when we were a child. But we may have a subtle feeling that something isn't right.

> *Balder's mother grounded herself through him. Her entire identity went through him, especially her grief, which was always deeper and more important than her son's joy, at least in her own eyes. The result was that Balder, often quite unconsciously, lived his life according to his mother's wishes.*

> *Finally, by using meditation to ground himself, not his mother, Balder regained authority over his life. His mother, on the other hand, felt very lonely, since all the support, i.e. grounding, she had had before was gone.*

Perhaps it seems strange that you can ground other people or be grounded through somebody else. If so, don't just go by what we say – do the next meditation and see what happens. During this meditation, it is vital that you are open to and accept any people you meet. Encounter them with acceptance and neutrality as regards yourself. Here again we will use tones to let go.

❦ MEDITATION ❦

MOVING OUT OTHER PEOPLE'S ENERGIES

Sit on a chair, close your eyes and take a few deep breaths.

Let your aura click into place at arm's length from your body.

Become aware of where you are present in your body.

Put one palm, or both, on your heart. Feel your heartbeat in your body.

Ask your heart if there is anything it wants to tell you right now.

Send a heartbeat down to the heart of the Earth and wait for the answer. Establish an energy exchange.

Send a new heartbeat down to the heart of the Earth. Let it pass through your body, down to the floor, through the floor, and so on. Stop if you encounter anybody or any form of resistance on your way.

Every time a person or form of resistance turns up:

Find a tone for the frequency that this person (or resistance) is stuck on. Sing it out. There is no point in doing it half-heartedly.

Find a tone that releases that person, or dissolves that resistance, and sing it at the top of your voice.

Finally, find a tone for your own frequency in this area.

Sing it out loud and clear and focus on what happens within.

Go to the next person or next resistance you encounter and repeat the tones until you have reached the heart of the Earth.

Let all you have experienced go down your grounding channel. Let go of it all.

Thank yourself for the steps you have taken. Thank your heart, your body and the Earth for the communication.

When you have finished, you may open your eyes.

Did you meet anyone in your grounding channel? Did you meet several people? Did you get to the heart of the Earth? It may be that someone you encountered wouldn't leave immediately. It doesn't matter if you feel they are still there, as you can do this meditation as often as you like. Finally they will let go and you will establish your own contact with the heart of the Earth.

Were you surprised by whom you met? From time to time, it's possible to believe that we're having problems with a certain person when we're really having problems with somebody else.

What if it was a special person who was stuck in your grounding channel in several places, perhaps your mother? You might have felt that you didn't want to let go of her, that it was wrong to force her to leave you. Maybe you thought that she'd always been there for you, so what right did you have to let her go?

The important thing in such a situation is to be aware that everybody has their own power. Everybody has the possibility of using this power. Whether you use it or not is completely your own choice. It is the same with the person you wish to remove. If you choose to let them go, do it with happiness and love for yourself and for them. Then the transitions will be smoother. If your mother, for example, doesn't quite accept that you're removing her from your grounding, she might get angry at you, without knowing why, or feel lonely, as in the story of Balder. It can be likened to getting heat from somebody else's fireplace. When your mother gets home, it will be very cold there. Perhaps she has even forgotten how to make her own fire.

Removing a person from your grounding is a powerful process and people around you might react to it. Be patient with them. Let them have their reaction. The fact that they have to start being grounded in themselves could lead to the very development they have tried to avoid. It could be difficult for them to have to shoulder the responsibility.

The reasons behind people's reactions can be complex. Sometimes it's a great relief to them that you've removed them. Your relations can improve. Suddenly you can meet as equals, and perhaps with a different perspective. Or they might not react at all. Again, there's no right or wrong here – it's your experience that counts.

Now that you own your grounding, the next step is to be conscious of it in your everyday life. It is great to be able to meditate and ground yourself in that way, but if you're only grounded then and at no other time in your life, you won't fully benefit from it. So, whenever you're stressed or feel insecure, irritated or indecisive, check your grounding. Do the simple exercise of letting your heart communicate with the heart of the Earth (*page 104*). In this way, you'll regain contact with the heart of the Earth, and your body and soul will automatically reconnect. You can also repeat any of the grounding exercises until you know you're grounded. Then you can start creating your life from a secure position.

The Foot Chakras

As well as having chakras, energy wheels, along our spine, we also have them on other places in our body, including our feet. Earth energy isn't only absorbed through our grounding channel, it is also absorbed through these chakras. They are placed right under the foot and can be experienced as energy gates. Just as we can pull and push our aura, so we can also open and close our chakras. All our chakras can be opened and closed through will power. If we imagine that our foot chakras are open, they are. This may sound too simple, but it really is easy and natural. We may know that our foot chakras are open by feeling warmth, prickling, or something similar right under our feet, or we may just know that they're open.

As well as grounding ourselves through meditation, we can also do so by walking in woods and fields. The following exercise offers you a chance to get grounded – through your feet.

❧ EXERCISE 4 ❧

CONSCIOUS WALKING

Go for a walk in a place you find beautiful – perhaps in a forest, in a park, by a lake or on a mountain.

Take a few deep breaths and become aware of where you are present in your body.

Are you only present in the upper part of your body? Are you present in your stomach? Or are you in touch with your legs?

Open your foot chakras by imagining that they are open. Feel the energy flow through your feet from the Earth.

Notice how your heel meets the ground. Do you put it down firmly or softly? What meets the ground first – your heel or another part of your foot?

Consider how the ground feels against your foot. Is it hard and cold or soft and welcoming, or something completely different?

As you walk, get in touch with your heart. Is there anything it wants to tell you?

Let a heartbeat go down to the heart of the Earth. Send another heartbeat down and wait for the response from the Earth. It might be an image, a tone, a feeling or an idea. Accept it.

Ask as many questions as you need. Every time you send a heartbeat down to the Earth, you will get an answer.

Feel how it affects your heart when you let your own energy and the Earth energy embrace there.

When the communication is established, focus on your legs again. How are they feeling right now?

Let energy flow from the Earth up through your feet. Make sure that your foot chakras are open by feeling warm or prickling sensations, or something similar, under your sole.

Every time you put down your foot, send resistance and anything else you want to get rid of, such as anger, grief, bitterness, judgement, of yourself or others, down to the Earth. Concentrate on letting it go through the grounding channel from your heart and your foot chakras.

Keep on walking for a while and send any resistance down through your heart and feet. Remember to breathe it out too.

When you feel that you've released everything, you can begin to receive new Earth energy every time you put your foot on the ground. Keep on walking for a while, receiving energy through your feet. Let it flow all the way up to your heart and merge with yours.

Then start releasing resistance when you put your right foot on the ground and receiving energy every time you put your left foot on the ground.

Keep on walking like this for a while, releasing with your right foot and receiving with your left foot.

Focus on what is going on in your body and remember to breathe.

When you feel that you have been walking in this way long enough, change sides. Receive energy with your right foot and release it away through your left foot.

Sense what is happening in your body this way round.

When you think you've been walking like this for long enough, let your body fall into its natural rhythm, receiving and releasing without trying to control it. Take in your surroundings and align your breathing to your natural pace.

Enjoy your walk!

In warm climates or when the weather permits, it may be a good idea to do this exercise barefoot. Your contact with the Earth will be even better, clearer and stronger when you do so. It is good to seek contact with the Earth. It is also great fun to walk consciously because there is a deeper dimension to it. Scents may become stronger, colours brighter, sounds louder, as though unconsciously all your senses are waking from slumber.

Through grounding, you basically make deeper contact with yourself. When you make this contact, you open up to the possibility of being in closer touch with your own truth. By being in close touch with your own truth, you can make loving decisions about your own life and when meeting others. In other words, when you are grounded, in whatever way works for you, you have the security to create your own life, not the life others would like you to lead.

Heavenly Grounding Food

Only you know what grounds you best. Whatever it is, it's enriching to find an activity that strengthens that connection. In this way, you can do your everyday chores and at the same time keep in conscious touch with yourself. We are both parents and like cooking. It grounds us. We find cooking some food types more grounding than others, especially lentils, beans and root vegetables, and would like to share some of our favourite recipes with you.

As already mentioned, everything has its own frequency. In the case of food, this frequency can be disturbed by the use of pesticides and packaging, and the way the food is harvested. This is why it's important to try to get hold of organic food, since it is closest to its original frequency. We can meditate as much as we like to raise our vibrational level, but if we keep eating unhealthy, spoiled, genetically modified food, our body won't be able to maintain that level for long. There's no need to be fanatical about food, however. Simply ask your heart what to eat or what your body wants right now and act upon it. You'll notice that you don't have to prevent yourself from eating unhealthy food; you simply won't crave it in the same way anymore. Communicate with your body and your heart, and do a 'healthy food search' for what you would like.

You might enjoy trying some of our recipes for heavenly grounding food.

Magic Grounding Bread

Makes two loaves

50g/1¾oz active yeast
1.3 litres/3 pints lukewarm water
1kg/2lb 4oz spelt flour, sifted
200g/7oz wholegrain spelt flour
2 tbsp unrefined sea salt
100g/3½oz oat flakes
100g/ 3½oz wheat bran
3 tbsp sunflower seeds
3 tbsp sesame seeds
3 tbsp linseeds

You may also add dried stinging nettles, nuts, psyllium, quinoa flour, soy flour, grated carrots, lentils, various sprouts, beans or other ingredients. There are infinite combinations.

Have you ever experienced bread dough bubbling while rising? Well, now you have the chance. The secret is to dissolve the yeast in water with your hands before you've touched the other ingredients. Pour the lukewarm water into a mixing bowl. Add the yeast and separate it with your hands till it is completely dissolved.

Add the dry ingredients and mix with a wooden spoon.

When the dough has the consistency of a mud pie, set it aside to rise. Let it rise for about 45 minutes, or until it has doubled in size.

Transfer the dough into two big loaf pans and place on the lowest rack in a cold oven. Bake at 180°C/350°F for 50 minutes. Alternatively, let the dough rise a second time for 45 minutes and then bake in a pre-heated oven at 200°C/400°F for 35–40 minutes.

Enjoy. *Bon appétit!*

Heavenly Lentil Soup

Serves 6

300g/10½oz dry green lentils
1.3 litres/3 pints water
2 vegetable stock cubes
2 onions, finely chopped
2 cloves garlic, finely chopped
2 tbsp ground cumin
4 tbsp soy sauce
salt and pepper
400ml/14fl oz can coconut milk

Put the lentils in the water with the vegetable stock cubes and bring to the boil.

Add the onions, garlic, cumin, soy sauce and pepper. Boil for about 20 minutes.

Add the coconut milk and simmer for about 10 minutes. Season to taste.

May be served with thin crispbread or rice. Boil the rice in its own saucepan and mix with the soup. (If it is boiled in the soup, you will have stewed lentils instead.)

Enjoy in the company of good friends.

Black-eyed Bean Risotto

Serves 6

10 sun-dried tomatoes
1kg/2lb 4oz brown rice, preferably basmati, boiled
500g/1lb 2oz black-eyed beans, boiled
    (from a can/carton or dried and boiled in advance)
4 tbsp butter-fried chanterelle mushrooms
2 tbsp pumpkin seeds
3 sprigs fresh coriander (cilantro)
zest of 2 lemons
zest of 1 lime
200–300g/7–10½oz mungo bean sprouts

For the dressing:
2–3 cloves garlic
100ml/3½fl oz good olive oil
juice of 1 lemon
juice of 1 lime
unrefined sea salt and freshly milled black pepper to taste

Prepare the sun-dried tomatoes by putting them in a bowl and pouring 100–200ml/3–7fl oz boiling water over them. Leave to draw while you prepare the other ingredients.

Mix the rice, beans, mushrooms, pumpkin seeds, coriander, lemon and lime zest and mungo bean sprouts in a bowl.

Prepare the dressing:
Crush the garlic in a pestle and mortar together with some flakes of unrefined salt. Slowly add the oil while stirring, then add the lemon and lime juice, salt and pepper.

Drain the tomatoes and dry them with kitchen paper. Chop them finely and fold them into the dressing.

Pour the dressing over the rice mixture and stir well.

Serve as a main course with crusty bread, or as a side dish.

A little magic tip: whenever you have rice for dinner, make sure to make a double portion so you have plenty of leftovers for making a scrumptious and grounding fast-food dinner the following night.

Enjoy!

Energy Sprouts

Growing sprouts is incredibly easy, fun and quite magical.

Take the beans, peas, lentils or seeds you wish to sprout and soak them in a glass jar overnight. Use a big jar, as they swell.

Pour out the water and rinse. Cover the top of the jar with a piece of cloth and secure it with an elastic band. Put the whole thing upside down at an angle in a bowl and leave in a dark place at room temperature, for instance in a cupboard.

Rinse the sprouts in cold water once a day. They are ready to eat when they have started sprouting. How long this takes varies quite a lot, depending on what beans and seeds you are sprouting. If you don't eat them at once, they can be left in the fridge for a couple of days.

Sprouts are one of the most potent foods you can have and can be served with everything. Use your wonderful imagination.

Angel Children

Serves 6

500g/1lb dried lima beans, soaked for at least 12 hours
cold water for cooking
1 tbsp of unrefined Atlantic sea salt
2 big sprigs fresh rosemary
150ml/5fl oz good-quality virgin olive oil

This is our favourite recipe.

Rinse the beans thoroughly under cold running water and transfer to a thick-bottomed saucepan. Add cold water to cover by a couple of centimetres (an inch).

Bring to the boil and when the water is foaming, add about 200ml/7fl oz cold water. Remove foam with a draining spoon or spoon.

Add salt, rosemary and olive oil. Simmer until beans are tender but not mushy.

Remove the saucepan from the heat and leave it to stand, preferably for a couple of hours, with the lid on.

After a good long rest, the beans will have absorbed both the flavour and fat from the salt, rosemary and olive oil, and you will understand why they are called both butter beans and angel children.

For a tasty variation, replace the lima beans with small white beans that have been soaked for at least two hours. Follow the recipe above and finally purée the beans. Delicious!

8

THE UNIVERSE

The importance of being grounded, of feeling we belong here on Earth, is vital. We need to take care of our body, both physically, through healthy eating, and energetically, through communication with the Earth. Even so, there may be something lacking, because the Earth is part of a bigger whole: the universe.

The physically perceived universe is comprised of endless space and planets. We need the sun for nutrients like vitamin D, and the moon steers all the cycles on Earth, including the tides and the cycles of both women and men, in addition to setting the standard for the calendar. We can also meet the universe on the subtle energy level through the universal power of love permeating and encompassing everything. You may call it God, the All, the One, the Divine, the Goddess, the universe or something similar. Even though it has many names, it is the same.

Imagine four people who have been sailing together all their lives. One day they are given the task of teaching others how to sail. They are going to teach separately on board the same boat they have been sailing for years and know from the inside out. However, even though they have been on the same boat, used with the same equipment and sailed in the same conditions, they will each have their unique experiences and ideas of what works for them. That is the reason why they will emphasize different aspects of sailing; four different sailing schools will develop.

The same goes for spiritual communication. We all speak about the same power. We simply experience it in different ways because of our individual points of view and experiences. So the next domain to enter, via our unique Spiritual Password, is the heart of the universe – the core of unconditional love.

Spiritual Contact

Spiritual contact is as important as grounding. By 'spiritual contact', we mean contact with the universal power of love within and around us. Still, before we establish such a contact, it is essential that the grounding is there as support and connection with the Earth and that we are present in our body. As we mentioned previously, we can choose to have spiritual contact only, but this is only half the story. We need the energy of the Earth to make inspiration and ideas manifest in the physical world.

Through the meditations of the previous chapters, hopefully you will have experienced grounding through making a connection between your heart and the heart of the Earth. Physically, the Earth doesn't have a heart as such, but a core of molten lava. However, we can encounter the heart of the Earth through meditation. In the next few meditations, we are going to work on the contact between our heart, the heart of the Earth and the heart of the universe. The same principle applies here: physically, we don't know there is such a centre, yet through meditation, using our double senses, we can encounter it. Just as we can communicate with the heart of the Earth, so we also can communicate with the heart of the universe through the Spiritual Password.

Grounding is our communication with the terrestrial spiritual world, and the contact with the heart of the universe is our communication with the universal spiritual world. It is through this contact that we have ideas and divine inspiration, and can encounter celestial beings such as angels. It is as if the universe has the seed of our existence and the Earth is the greenhouse. As they work together, we are nurtured like a living plant that needs sun and warmth from the universe as well as soil and water from the Earth.

❦ MEDITATION ❦

FINDING THE SPIRITUAL PASSWORD TO THE HEART OF THE UNIVERSE

Sit on a chair, close your eyes and take a few deep breaths.

Let your aura click into place at arm's length from your body.

Become aware of where you are present in your body.

Breathe out any resistance you encounter and breathe in more of yourself and your own energy.

Put one of your palms, or both, on your heart and become aware of your heartbeat against your palm.

Send a heartbeat to the heart of the Earth and wait for the response.

Give and receive with every heartbeat. Feel your energy and the energy of the Earth merge in your heart.

Send a heartbeat to the heart of the universe. Let it travel up through your chest, throat and head and out through the ceiling, and perhaps other floors, and then straight to the heart of the universe.

Breathe out any old images of the universe without a centre, and find the Spiritual Password to the heart of the universe: see the heart of the universe, feel the heart of the universe, experience it as a tone or a colour, know it is there or simply feel it in your unique way.

Focus on your heart again. Let a heartbeat go straight to the heart of the universe without following it.

Be consciously present in your heart and start being aware of the response from the heart of the universe in your heart. It can be a returning heartbeat, warmth or coldness, a tone, a feeling, a colour or something completely different. Receive your unique Spiritual Password with acceptance and love for yourself.

Remain seated for a while, sending energy to the heart of the universe and receiving it back. Feel how it affects your heart when your own energy, the energy of the Earth and the energy of the universe merge there.

Become aware of the energy pillar you have created from the heart of the universe via your heart to the heart of the Earth. Heaven and Earth meet in you when communication is flowing through the pillar. Every heartbeat spreads upwards and downwards from your heart, just like ripples spreading out on water. The only thing you need to do for this to happen is to be present in your heart. Just know that every heartbeat goes to the heart of the Earth and to the heart of the universe. Receive answers from both in your heart simultaneously.

Let go of your feelings, resistance or tones – everything you have encountered during the meditation – and send them down your grounding channel.

Thank yourself for the steps you've taken, and thank your heart, the Earth and the universe for the communication.

When you have finished, you may open your eyes.

Did you manage to encounter the heart of the universe without judgement? If you did, great, and if you didn't – great! Both experiences are information for you about your unique contact with the universal power of love. It is different for everybody, just as grounding differs for everybody. Did you see a colour, did you hear a tone, did you experience a feeling or did you experience something completely different? Remember that it's your own Spiritual Password that you are exploring and everything is of equal value.

Your Unique Connection with the Heart of the Universe

Perhaps it has been a long time since you had your own unique communication with the heart of the universe. Maybe you met someone you knew on the way there. Other people may have decided what your communication with the spiritual world should be like. Could others know best?

Let's do an experiment. Imagine that you have a crush on somebody, but someone else tells you that what you're feeling isn't really a crush. Suppose they claim that you have to have a pulse of 220 beats per minute, blush every time the person is within sight, sweat so much that you drop whatever you're holding and tremble so much that people next to you can hear your knees knocking before it qualifies as a true crush. This could lead to one of two outcomes: either you tell them, 'That's nonsense – I want to keep on trusting my own impulses and feelings,' or you listen to them and doubt your own experience.

We believe in our own experiences when it comes to having a crush on someone. But many of us have learned that other people know more about how our contact with the universal power of love, or God, should be than we do.

The important thing is that it is possible for each and every one of us to have our own hotline to Heaven – in our own way. With our own experiences. The following excerpt of a story from Selma Lagerlöf's *The Angel by the Apal Crescent*, illustrates this:

The Shepherd's Prayer

A young shepherd is speaking to God from his heart. He shows how dearly he loves God by comparing Him with a lamb or a wolf, but he doesn't kneel down or light any candles.

One day a scholar is passing by and sees the shepherd speaking to God. He explains to him that praying is an art. 'You have to light a candle,' he says, 'clasp your hands, read the scriptures and kneel.'

From that day on, the shepherd stops praying.

One night the scholar has a dream in which a voice says, 'Do you want to take away an innocent child's prayers from me? The shepherd wasn't a scholar and didn't know any difficult words, but he prayed with his heart and now I miss his prayers every day.'

The scholar immediately sets off to find the shepherd and asks if he can pray for them both. 'Dear God,' he says, without lighting a candle and without kneeling down, 'if I were a shepherd I would speak to you from my heart. And I wouldn't let anybody stop me: not a lamb, not a wolf and not a self-righteous old man.'

If you set aside your way of communicating with the universal power of love and use that of others instead, you're actually saying that your way isn't good enough. You're giving away your own energy and placing other people's energies – that is to say, other people's experiences and solutions – above your own. We believe that it's possible for everybody to have their own particular contact with the heart of the universe, just as it's possible for everyone to have their own unique contact with the heart of the Earth. It is vital that everyone does what is right for them.

We have different needs in this area too. There are people who need the security they get from somebody telling them how to communicate with the Godhead. There are people who need to go through a guru or a spiritual master. Both are of equal value. The essential thing is not which choice you make, but being aware of the choice.

Nobody's truth is more important than anyone else's. If you have a special way of encountering the universal power of love and you don't wish to change it, that's perfectly alright. On the other hand, if you encounter some people on your way to the heart of the universe, or you feel that your heartbeats don't get all the way there, then maybe you should work on removing some blockages from your pillar of communication. Again, you can do this by means of tones.

❦ MEDITATION ❦

MOVING OUT OTHER PEOPLE'S ENERGIES

Sit on a chair, close your eyes and take a few deep breaths.

Let go of what you have just done and what you are about to do, and become present.

Let your aura click into place at arm's length from your body.

Become aware of where you are present in your body.

Breathe out resistance and breathe in more of yourself and your own energy.

Put one of your palms, or both, on your heart. Become aware of the heartbeat in your body.

Ask your heart if there is anything it wants to tell you right now.

Send a heartbeat to the centre of the Earth and receive the response in your heart. Establish an energy flow from the heart of the Earth to your heart and let the two energies merge in your heart.

Now, still present in your heart, send a heartbeat to the heart of the universe and wait for the response. It may be an image, a tone, a feeling or an impulse. Receive it in your heart and let the three energies blend in your heart.

Send a new heartbeat to the heart of the universe. Let it pass through your chest, throat, head, the roof, and so on.

Stop if you encounter anyone or any resistance on the way, and do the following:

Find a tone for the frequency where this person/ resistance is stuck. Sing it out. There is no point in doing it half-heartedly.

Find a tone for releasing the person or the resistance. Sing it at the top of your voice.

Finally, find the tone of your own frequency in the area. Sing it loud and clear and focus on what's going on in your body.

Let your heartbeat continue towards the heart of the universe. When you meet another person or more resistance, repeat the tones. Continue until you've reached the very heart of the universe.

Focus on your heart again. With every heartbeat, energy leaves you and returns to you, going to the heart of the universe and the heart of the Earth and back at the same time. Stay present in your heart and feel how this affects you. Let the energy of the Earth and the energy of the universe merge with you and your own unique essence.

Enjoy this for a few minutes.

Let go of everything you have encountered during the meditation – feelings, resistance, tones – and send it down your grounding channel.

Thank yourself for the steps you've taken, and thank your heart, the Earth and the universe for the communication.

When you have finished, you may open your eyes.

Did you encounter anybody on your way to the heart of the universe? Maybe it was somebody you knew would be there, or maybe it was a different person. Was it a relief to let go of them or was it painful? Perhaps they refused to let go. Remember that at some point or other, you chose to have them there, perhaps because you said no to your own information and yes to someone else's.

There are many people who consciously or unconsciously can't stand other people's light. Perhaps they've rejected their own truth and therefore can't allow others to have theirs. It's too painful to be reminded of the sacrifice they once made. So they prevent others around them from standing shining in their own truth. But remember – you aren't a child anymore. You can make decisions without relying on the people around you. You can choose to take charge of your life right now, without taking into account those who are holding you back. You can choose to be free because you are conscious of your Spiritual Password to the heart of the universe.

Our Deepest Fear

Our deepest fear is not that we are inadequate. Our deepest fear is that we are powerful beyond measure. It is our light, not our darkness, that most frightens us. We ask ourselves: Who am I to be brilliant, gorgeous, talented, fabulous? Actually, who are you not to be? You are a child of God.

Your playing small does not serve the world. There is nothing enlightened about shrinking so that other people won't feel insecure around you. We are all meant to shine, as children do. We were born to make manifest the glory of God that is within us. It's not just in some of us: it's in everyone. And as we let our own light shine, we unconsciously give other people permission to do the same. As we are liberated from our own fear, our presence automatically liberates others.

MARIANNE WILLIAMSON

9

$\mathcal{T}$HE BEST THING IN LIFE

Growing up, we learn various skills such as walking, climbing, writing, playing a certain sport, and so on. We learn how to take care of ourselves, so we know our physical limits and abilities. These are all skills of the physical realm and we don't get the same education in our non-physical part – the subtle energy field that surrounds us. How does this affect us? Knowing how to be present in life under all circumstances is, of course, exceptionally important, and we may be aided in being conscious in life through clicking our aura into place, being grounded and communicating with the heart of the universe. Yet we often lose out on having an even energy level throughout the day. This is one of the most important secrets we teach our students: how to give to ourselves.

Some people believe it is selfish to think of ourselves first. When we set aside our own needs, we are often seen as self-sacrificing and unselfish. Still, nobody fills up their car with petrol before a long drive and then gives petrol from their own tank to five other cars before departure.

Everyone understands that their car won't get very far if they do this. It's exactly the same with our energy. If we give it to everybody else without giving to ourselves, we won't last very long. We may keep going for a while, a few years perhaps, but finally we'll run on empty.

Just as the body provides itself with nutrition through the blood, so we give our body nutrition through the subtle energies. That's why it's important to know how to give your body this kind of nutrition continuously. The next meditation will show you how. When you get used to doing this meditation, you can do it wherever you are: on the bus, at the shops, at the hairdresser's, in the shower or while you're waiting for the traffic lights to turn green.

❦ MEDITATION ❦

GIVING TO YOURSELF

Sit on a chair, close your eyes and take a few deep breaths.

Let go of what you have just done and what you are about to do, and become present.

Let your aura click into place at arm's length from your body.

Become aware of where you are present in your body.

Put one of your palms, or both, on your heart.

Ask your heart if there is anything it wants to tell you right now.

Send a heartbeat down to the heart of the Earth and receive the response in your heart. Remember that there is a constant energy exchange between the heart of the Earth and your heart.

Now send a heartbeat to the heart of the universe and wait for the response in your heart. Remember that there is a constant energy exchange between the heart of the universe and your heart.

Become aware of how your unique energy merges with the Earth energy and the universal energy in your heart. Feel how the communication between your heart, the heart of the Earth and the heart of the universe join to form a pillar creating wholeness, a connection between Heaven and Earth with your heart as the link.

Now let the three energies blend as one in the source of your heart and flow over and fill your heart.

When it is full, let the energies flow into your body and fill every cell from the bone marrow to the outer skin layer.

Just receive the energies.

When your body is full, let the energies flow into your aura and fill it.

When the aura is full, let the energies overflow along the edge of your aura, cleansing it, and then down your grounding channel to the heart of the Earth.

Remain present in your heart and let your infinite source, which communicates with the Earth and the universe, feed your heart, your body and your aura. Let the energy surplus continue to flow along the edge of your aura and down your grounding channel to the heart of the Earth.

While you are letting the energies flow around your body and aura, your heart is communicating with the heart of the Earth and the heart of the universe. Remain present in your heart and give to yourself for a while.

When you give to yourself in this way, feelings, incidents, resistance and other things may emerge in your consciousness. Take whatever comes into your heart and send it down your grounding channel, while remembering to breathe out everything that enters your awareness and breathe in more of yourself and your energy.

THE BEST THING IN LIFE

Focus on your heart again, which is still communicating with the heart of the Earth and the heart of the universe. Intend to keep on giving to yourself when you have come out of meditation.

Thank yourself for the steps you have taken.

Thank your body, the Earth and the universe for the gifts they have brought you.

When you have finished, you may open your eyes.

Could you give to yourself with ease? Or was it difficult to receive? Did any parts of your body have more difficulty receiving than others? Did you meet any people during your meditation who told you that what you were doing wasn't allowed? If so, you now have the tools both to address any resistance in yourself and to move other people's energies out of your body or aura. You can either breathe out the resistance and/or people while you are breathing in more of yourself and your own energy, or you can use tones (find a tone for the frequency the person/resistance is stuck on, find a tone for letting go and find a tone for your own energy frequency in this area).

It is good to repeat this meditation before you continue. That way you'll get a better grasp of the procedure. Remember you can do the meditation anywhere. 'No way,' you may say, 'it took half an hour to do.' If we'd needed half an hour every time we were going to give to ourselves, we wouldn't have carried on either. The thing is, when you've done this meditation several times, it'll only take a few seconds to get into the flow and you can give yourself a quick fix.

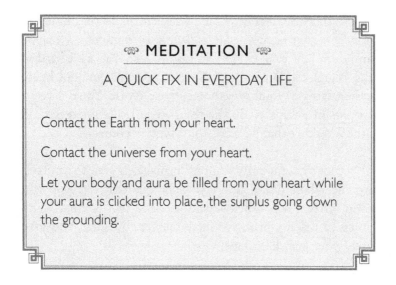

❀ **MEDITATION** ❀

A QUICK FIX IN EVERYDAY LIFE

Contact the Earth from your heart.

Contact the universe from your heart.

Let your body and aura be filled from your heart while your aura is clicked into place, the surplus going down the grounding.

So you see it's very quick: smack, smack, smack.

Do this meditation till you feel you've mastered doing it quickly. It doesn't matter whether it takes three times or three weeks. Give yourself the time you need without speeding it up. Allow yourself to do it at your own pace.

Then, when you are out in the real world, you can concentrate for a couple of minutes to get into the flow and give to yourself, for example, on the bus on your way to work. You can also take a few minutes in the locker room or at your own office, before you meet other people. Focus on being in communication with the centre of the Earth and the universe from your heart, and give to yourself. Remain in this flow when you meet others. See what happens.

The real trick is keeping the energy flow going all day, being present in your life and giving vital new energy to yourself all the time. So, feel how long you manage to remain in the flow. Do you manage only a couple of minutes, or maybe an hour? Is it easy or do you lose focus? It is a bit hard in the beginning, but it's worth practising. Imagine not being exhausted on your way home from work. You'd have a surplus of energy to do the things you really appreciate in life. Wouldn't that be a great gift to give yourself?

Don't lose courage if you don't manage to give to yourself for the whole day. There is a technique that can help you even further. It is called separation, and that is what we're going to teach you in the final chapter. But first, you may greet your guardian angel.

10

$\mathscr{A}$NGELS

Until now, we have explored the Spiritual Password purely in regard to ourselves, our energetic connections to our heart, the Earth and the universe. But we can also find the Spiritual Password to anything we choose on the spiritual web. In the same way that we can search for a certain topic on the web, we can also choose to contact various aspects of the spiritual web, such as our guides or animal guides.

The choice of connection is up to you, but since working with the pure energy of angels is our speciality, we will enlighten you now on how to find the Spiritual Password to your guardian angel.

Angels are loving celestial beings found in all religions. The word 'angel' is derived from the Greek word *angelos*, which means 'harbinger' or 'messenger'. A characteristic feature of angels is that they have wings. In Christian and Jewish tradition, there are archangels, seraphim, cherubim, and ordinary angels. Islam has basically the same classifications: *hamalat al-Arsh*, *karibuyin* and archangels. Angels are also present in Hinduism and Buddhism, though in a different form. We also find them in the ancient religions of Egypt, where the gods are portrayed with wings. In the ancient Persian religion of Zoroastrianism, angels were called *amesha spentas* and *yazatas*. The Zoroastrians have additional creatures that resemble guardian angels, namely *fravashis*. This phenomenon is also found in Roman myths, where each person has a guardian spirit: Juno for women and Genius for men. In Islam, every person has a guardian angel, one for enumerating good deeds and another for enumerating bad deeds.

Saying a Heartfelt 'Yes' to Angels

Every angel reflects an aspect of universal love – a component, a part, of God. It is as easy for us to encounter angels as it is to communicate with our heart, simply because it is natural for us to do so. But just as we tend to shut off the communication with our body or heart, so we can also close off the Spiritual Password to angels and lose the dialogue with them. But angels are there for us, no matter what, whether we close off communication or not. They can help us to get to know ourselves better. They can help us find our way so we can live our life with happiness and love. They can help us find the way to our own greatness, to our true essence – to unconditional love.

Only we can prevent ourselves from getting in touch with angels. If we choose to say yes to their participation in our life, then we will have answers from them. It really has to be a heartfelt yes, but if you really mean it, truly and honestly, you will be answered before you know it.

❦ MEDITATION ❦

INVITING ANGELS INTO YOUR LIFE

Close your eyes and contact your heart. Let your heart contact the Earth and the universe and fill your body and aura with their merging energies.

Say a heartfelt yes to angels participating in your life from now on. Ask if they can give you a sign of their presence. Say yes to being open to understanding the answer they bring, however it comes to you.

Thank the angels for always being with you.

Thank yourself for being open and receptive to the communication with them.

Finding the Spiritual Password to your Guardian Angel

Finding the Spiritual Password to communicating with angels is a bit more challenging than discovering the Spiritual Password to, for instance, your heart. Finding the Spiritual Password to your heart is an inner search, where the password comes solely from your heart in various forms. As angels exist independently of us, they can answer us by letting something emerge from within, by letting a certain vibration resonate in us, as we have encountered in previous chapters, but they can just as easily provide an answer in the outer world. It could be something we happen to read in a paper. It could be something somebody says to us. It might be something we hear on the radio, something we see on television, something we'd forgotten then suddenly recall, or it might be a feather suddenly appearing under our nose, once or maybe several times. So, being present in everyday life is rather important. If we aren't, the moment might pass us by, and we might remain under the illusion that we're not in contact with angels. This is the reason for finding the Spiritual Password on all levels of our own energetic body first: so that we start becoming conscious as we journey through life.

It may be that we receive a response, but our common sense tries to tell us that it's just a coincidence. That's absolutely right. It *is* a coincidence – a divine coincidence. In our experience, divine coincidences are never coincidental.

So, allow yourself to have an open mind. Don't reason away your experience, don't let reason tear it into pieces and don't end up believing that nothing has happened. Let the experience remain an experience. Dare to see what happens when you aren't in absolute control of your life and are alert to the divine coincidences you will encounter. Perhaps they will take you to a place you have wanted to go for a long time.

Angels communicate with us in as many ways as there are people on Earth. Just as we have our own unique Spiritual Password to our body, our heart, the Earth and the universe, so we have our own unique Spiritual Password to angels.

Angels come in different shapes and sizes, and they are an aspect of unconditional love (i.e., God) without physical structure. Each and every angel therefore has its own power frequency. A frequency can be transformed into light, sound, feeling, colour, smell or taste, so every angel has a particular light, sound, feeling, colour, smell and taste that it can resonate within you so that you perceive it with your double senses.

Everyone who encounters this aspect of universal love does so from their own starting point and with their own baggage of past experiences. This is the reason why we perceive the same aspect of the universal love – or the same angel – differently. Suppose we were to ask several people what they associated with the colour red; some would say 'love' or 'passion', others 'war' or 'bloodbath', yet others 'tomato', 'anger', 'aggression' or 'mother's nail varnish'. Yet all the various answers are associated with the same colour. It's the same with angels too. The same angel – the same divine frequency – may be perceived in various forms, colours and ways. So please don't be alarmed if you perceive your guardian angel in a different way from what you expect or what you have read in books. It is perfectly fine. Just allow yourself to be in the now and accept the experience instead of mentally controlling or judging it. You are unique, so your encounter with your guardian angel will be unique too.

The less you know about the angel you are to encounter, the better. Then you won't have to plough through the information other people have given you. As with your other encounters – with your body, your heart, the Earth and the universe – other people's thoughts and patterns may govern your perceptions of how you can meet angels and who they are. But nobody, apart from you, knows who your guardian angel is.

The forms in which angels appear are unlimited. You might perceive angels as a light, in human shape, in animal shape, as angels on a scrap of paper, or as a smell, or you may get a tingling in your body, get goose bumps, feel you just know what they are saying to you or simply be aware of a loving presence. It's worth repeating that every Spiritual Password is unique. Our own will manifest in such a way that we can receive it the very second we encounter it.

MÄRTHA:
I have no childhood memories of beating, protective wings indicating that my guardian angel was near. My first conscious encounter with an angel took place as an adult while reading a book called Ask Your Angels. I'd tried for a long time to fit into the 'normal box'. Being a princess and having spiritual gifts put me in quite a difficult spot in this respect, and I fought hard for a place in the 'sought-after box'. Through the encounter with my guardian angel, everything changed; when my guardian angel entered the room, I noticed the smell of roses and felt a strong and loving presence. The presence was so profound that I couldn't act as though I wasn't aware of it, and I accepted there and then that these kinds of experiences were

*normal to me. After that, I started trusting my own judgement
and what my heart told me. My creativity skyrocketed and
slowly but steadily I changed from being a full-time equestrian
to being a spiritual teacher, writing books and giving talks and
workshops all over the world.*

Some people have an enlightening experience meeting an
angel for the first time, and that's great. But for most of us,
the first encounter may, for example, be just a soft touch
on the left shoulder, feeling a loving presence in the room
or getting a tingling sensation. Our life doesn't have to
change dramatically either, not there and then. But, as in
the story above, acknowledging who we are and recognizing
our spiritual greatness will change our life. We might not
feel the change at all, but listening to our heart and shifting
our awareness from trying to run away from walking our
spiritual path to actually being proud of having this in our
life, will in time change that life.

As angels are an aspect of universal love (i.e., unconditional
love) in balance, and therefore have their masculine
and feminine energy in complete equilibrium, they are
androgynous. Consequently it is possible for two people to
perceive the same angel as having a different gender – one
may perceive it as masculine, the other may perceive it as
feminine. Since angels are androgynous, we can also perceive
them as both masculine and feminine at the same time – their
image may be indecisively masculine or feminine, or we may
sense the angel's front as feminine and its back as masculine,
or the other way around.

Angels have no egos, again because they are an aspect
of universal love. So, if we feel that they are sad or
disappointed by something we do, we are only seeing them

through our own ego structure and our own feelings. How can they be disappointed in us when they regard us from the perspective of our divine power – our highest potential? Angels will always see us through the eyes of divine love, and accordingly they will only see us in our greatness. They will remind us of who we actually are, under all the fear and misconceptions of ourselves that make us live out only a small part of who we truly are. If we see ourselves through their eyes, we can love ourselves as they love us.

Angels are there for all of us. The point is that we have to get in touch with them. We have the free will to lead our life just as we choose. If we decide that our life is better without angels in it, the angels will respect that and won't take an active part in it. If, on the contrary, we change our thought pattern and invite angels into our life, they will be more than happy to assist us in whatever way they can. Mind you, even if you deliberately block them out of your life, they will still be there with you. Your guardian angel is always there for you.

There are endless numbers of angels. The fact that only a few of them are named and known to us doesn't mean there aren't more of them. During the past few years, people have become more open about describing encounters with angels. Many have been in touch with angels and told their stories.

Does everyone really have a guardian angel? Yes, they do. Our guardian angel is there to reflect who we are, so that we will always be aware of our own power and greatness. Our guardian angel is there as a warm reminder to look upon ourselves with love, so that we create our life out of love for ourselves, thus being there for others on our conditions.

Our guardian angel is a support in life, one who – if we permit – always paves the way for us. One who makes life go like clockwork so that we are in the right place at the right time and meet the people we need to meet for the next step of our life project.

ELISABETH:

> As long as I can remember, I have felt a presence around me. In my childhood I had a close friend whom I called 'the Girl'. I played with her and talked with her, and I perceived her as a loving protection that gave me security. The adults around me were very understanding about my make-believe friend. But when I got older, that understanding from those around me vanished. In order to adjust to my surroundings, I had to shut off my communication with the Girl. Only as an adult did I dare to encounter this wonderful, loving energy, my guardian angel.

Some people might think that it's difficult to encounter their guardian angel. They might not think that they're worthy of this divine contact. Perhaps they have more faith in other people's opinions than in this aspect of the Divine. It will demand something of you as a human, and it will demand something of your soul to give yourself permission to encounter angels. You will get that permission only when you dare to encounter the greatness within yourself.

The paradox is that often what we are looking for, for example our true potential, is what we fear most of all. Suppose you get what you wish for – whom will you put the blame on then? Having angels in your life means taking a firmer grip on your own life, taking full responsibility. It is about trusting yourself so you dare to live your dream. You know deep down that you have the map to find the road ahead. Angels are loving and wise life companions. Maybe the time has come for you to take charge of your own life.

When you re-establish the Spiritual Password to your guardian angel – 're-establish' because again we are bold enough to say that you had this contact before – it is important that you know that whatever happens, the experience is real for you. It will be characterized by where you are in life – by the baggage you bring to this moment. Here again, there are different ways of perceiving the Spiritual Password. Some people notice a smell. Others feel a breeze against their brow, cheek or some other part of their body. Some feel a light touch. Others see shapes. Some see colours. Others hear tones or an angelic choir. Some feel a tingling of the skin. Others just know that their guardian angel is present. Maybe you experience combinations of these. There is no rule book – only your experience. Allow yourself to totally accept yourself and whatever happens.

❦ MEDITATION ❦

ENCOUNTERING YOUR GUARDIAN ANGEL THROUGH THE SPIRITUAL PASSWORD

Sit on a chair, close your eyes and take a few deep breaths.

Let go of what you have just done and what you are about to do and become present. Let your aura click into place.

Place one of your palms, or both, on your heart. Ask your heart if there is anything it wants to tell you right now.

Contact the Earth from your heart, contact the universe from your heart and let the three energies merge in your heart, giving to yourself.

Begin to become aware of your guardian angel. Where are they in relation to you? Are they in front of you, behind you or beside you? Are they close or far away?

Ask your guardian angel to stand right in front of you and slowly turn around so you can perceive it from all angles.

Find the Spiritual Password to your guardian angel. What colour is your guardian angel? Is it feminine, masculine or perhaps both at once? Does it have a tone? Do you get a certain feeling? Do you sense a smell? Or do you simply know that your guardian angel is there?

From your heart, ask if there is anything your guardian angel wants to tell you right now and receive their response in whatever form it may surface.

Be aware of whether your guardian angel is holding something in one or both hands – or is not holding anything at all. If your guardian angel is holding something, ask from your heart how to use it – and again, receive the answer in your unique way.

Finally, ask your guardian angel how and when you best can communicate with them.

Thank your guardian angel for the encounter and let go of what you have experienced, but know that your guardian angel will always be with you.

Remain conscious in your heart and make communication with the Earth and the universe.

Fill your heart, body and aura with revitalizing energy and let the surplus go down to the centre of the Earth.

Intend to keep on giving to yourself when you come out of meditation.

Thank yourself, your body and your heart for the steps you have taken.

When you have finished, you may open your eyes.

Was it surprisingly easy to re-establish the Spiritual Password to your guardian angel, or was it hard? Did you feel that you didn't experience anything? Or maybe the impressions were so strong that you were overwhelmed? Or was it something in between? Remember that this was your unique encounter with your guardian angel. So, accept what happened. Whatever it was, it was perfect, as it told you something about where you are in life.

To some, this encounter will seem familiar and close, as if they have lost contact with a good friend who suddenly turns up in their life again, and they only now understand how much they've missed them. For others, their guardian angel may appear as a new acquaintance. What if you didn't experience anything at all? That's OK. Perhaps you still knew that your guardian angel was there. Perhaps you knew what it looked like. Perhaps you even *pretended* to know what it looked like. That is also fine. Everything goes. The important thing is for you to trust whatever comes to you. Whatever it is, it's good enough. You have your way of communicating, others have theirs. Trust yourself and accept that you have been in touch with your guardian angel.

Some people get sceptical at this point and say, 'What if I met an angel of darkness? How do we know that the angels we meet are the real thing?' If you feel you have met an angel of darkness or an evil force, be sure that this is *not* your guardian angel. Darkness is solely an absence of light. Just as the sun can't exist in the shadows, angels can't exist in darkness, as they are an aspect of unconditional love, i.e., pure light. When you contact them from a conscious, open heart, you can't go wrong. The above meditation is a 100 per cent safe way of contacting your guardian angel. If you don't meet the angelic realm of love doing the meditation, you simply haven't met an angel. What can you do then? Let go of your fears. What situation or person created this fear of meeting an evil force? Why do you believe that you aren't worthy of the love of angels? Whenever we doubt angels, this reflects something within us. When you manage to let go of the fear holding you back, your true connection with the angelic realm will emerge and you will make a loving connection with your guardian angel.

Maybe you met a deceased loved one when contacting your guardian angel. That is OK too. A lot of people have deceased loved ones as protectors who counsel and guide them on their way. Just know that a deceased loved one is different from a guardian angel. Although deceased loved ones have a different frequency from angels, there is no problem having contact with them as well as your guardian angel. The important thing is to be conscious of the difference so that you may recognize an angel when you meet one. Deceased loved ones have been physically on the planet and therefore have an ego. Angels have not been physically on Mother Earth and therefore do not have an ego.

If you met a deceased loved one during the meditation, maybe it was important for you to know that they were with you. Maybe they had a certain message for you that was important. Now you have most likely received that message through the meditation, you can move on to the angels.

Next time you do the meditation, ask your deceased loved one from your open loving heart to step aside so that you may meet your guardian angel. If they don't step aside, it means that they are blocking your way to the angels. This is not solely their fault. Maybe it has been necessary to block your contact with your angels for a period of time. Maybe this kind of connection wasn't accepted when you were growing up. Your deceased loved one may have actually done you a favour by protecting you from making contact with angels. But you might be in a different situation in your life now, one where you can have this contact freely. So, feel where your loved one is attached to your body and use the tones to let go with love: find a tone for the person blocking your way to the angels, find a tone to let go, thank this person for having helped you in a certain phase of your life and let them walk out of the door. Then find a tone for your true vibration in that area of your body. Now do the meditation again and see if anything has changed or not.

Angels want us to be happy and create our lives in a light but still profound manner by living consciously. When we are conscious, we are able to take responsibility for our emotions and reactions, because we are always seeking to find the cause of our various reactions within. When we are oblivious to a certain pattern, we cannot for the life of us do anything about it, because we simply don't know about it. But when we're conscious of this pattern, we suddenly get a choice and can ask ourselves: 'Do I want this pattern in my life or not?'

If you don't want a particular pattern in your life, let it go. Every time you let go of something that isn't your essence, you make even more room for the true, loving you. When you start taking responsibility in your life, you suddenly stop blaming everybody else for what is happening or how you are feeling, because you know that you can do something about it, namely let go of whatever is causing the reaction or triggering the pattern in you. You can't change anybody else, but you can change the way you encounter them. With the help of angels, this process will be much smoother. All you have to do is ask from your heart and let the angels do their work.

Contact from your Heart

In addition to giving you hints and impulses for your everyday life, your guardian angel can help you to get rid of old memories, patterns and emotional knots that are still affecting you. There may be irritating everyday incidents and other things you want to let go. This meditation works in the same way as the communication with the Earth. By establishing a contact from your heart to your guardian angel's heart, you can send away unwanted energy and get back divine love.

❧ MEDITATION ❧

LETTING GO WITH HELP FROM
YOUR GUARDIAN ANGEL

Sit on a chair, close your eyes and take a few deep breaths.

Let go of what you have just done and what you are about to do, and become present.

Let your aura click into place. Become aware of where you are in your body.

Put one of your palms, or both, on your heart.

Ask your heart if there is anything it wants to tell you right now.

Contact the Earth and contact the universe from your heart and let the three energies merge in your heart.

Let your body and aura be filled from your heart and let the surplus go down to the heart of the Earth. Give to yourself for a while and send whatever surfaces in your mind down the grounding channel.

Ask your guardian angel to stand in front of you.

Focus on your heart and simply let it show you a colour or a light. Allow this shining colour or light to radiate from your heart to meet the heart of your guardian angel. This will create a conscious strengthening of the connection between you and your guardian angel.

Sit there receiving the energy flowing from your guardian angel.

In the same way that a pulse, a rhythm, is created in the pillar of energetic exchange between the Earth and the universe with your heart at the centre, a flow of energy is now being created between you and your guardian angel.

Notice if the connection between you and your guardian angel is thinner in the middle, or if some places are thinner than others. Let go of resistance by breathing it out and breathing in more of yourself and your energy, and let the connection expand.

Ask your heart if there is anything you are ready to let go of.

If there is, send it away from your heart and let it travel along the ray from your heart to the heart of your guardian angel.

Know that angels transform everything in love and gratitude, and they want to give energy, filled with love, back to you. So, remain in the flow in an exchange of energies – letting go and receiving a response from your guardian angel in return.

Thank yourself for the steps you've taken, and thank your guardian angel for the encounter.

Release your guardian angel, but know that it is always there for you.

Be present in your heart and make communication with the Earth and the universe.

Fill your heart, body and aura with revitalizing energy
and let the surplus go down to the centre of the Earth.
Intend to keep on giving to yourself when you have
come out of the meditation.

Thank your body and your heart for the steps you've
taken.

When you have finished, you may open your eyes.

Now you can re-establish contact with your guardian angel
whenever you want to. It is as easy to speak to your guardian
angel as it is to communicate with your heart, because you
have now mastered the secret of the Spiritual Password.

You can communicate with your guardian angel at any
place and any time. You can do it by following the previous
meditations or in your own special way. When you are
ready to embark on your own journey of life, with your own
power and your unique potential at the centre of it, let the
angels be there.

The essential thing is that you now take your guardian angel
with you in life. You now listen and are sensitive to signs. You
now live in gratitude and allow yourself to live your life out
of love for yourself. When you live your life out of love for
yourself, you wish only the best for yourself, meaning you live
in harmony with others. Thus you manifest a life that brings
good experiences to you, both on your own and together with
others. In other words, you have the life you wish for.

You have now mastered the Spiritual Password and can find whatever you wish on the spiritual web, contact it through your heart and access it via the Spiritual Password. Have fun with the password, enjoy it, but be true to your heart, your grounding and your connection to the universe as well as to your guardian angel. Enjoy being conscious in your life. Enjoy being you to the full.

EVENING PRAYER

When I lay me down to sleep

thirteen angels by me stand;

two upon my right hand side,

two upon my left hand glide

two stand watch by my cushion,

two at my feet as conclusion,

two to tuck me,

two to wake me,

one to open my eyes

to all of Heaven's paradise.

HENRIK WERGELAND (1808–45)

11

$\mathcal{S}$EPARATING

Now we're almost at the end of our journey together – *almost*. We have one more meditation. This is such an amazingly good technique that we have to share it with you. It is a wonderful help if you are the least bit hypersensitive, taking in other people's emotions and thinking they are your own, getting drained from being with other people and not knowing how to protect yourself. It can help you leave your work where it belongs – at work – instead of bringing it home. And you can keep your energy levels up in spite of giving to others all day.

The meditation is so simple that anybody can do it and so efficient that we believe it should be compulsory for everyone who deals with people. It is as efficient for the healer as it is for the hairdresser, for the waiter as it is for the bus driver, for the shop assistant as it is for the teacher, for the flight attendant as it is for the doctor. Why? Because it helps us take what is ours and what we've given away during the treatment, the class or the course of the day – namely, our own energy. It also makes it possible for us to give back what we've taken from others, that is to say, their energy.

Energy Givers and Energy Takers

We are constantly exchanging energy with other people. When we socialize, we give and take. We do it more or less unconsciously. We experience some people as energy givers – they often make us excited, keen and happy. We experience other people as energy takers – they often make us weak and low. Sometimes an energy exchange results in more energy for everyone, for example in a meeting. Then everyone has an energy boost, gets inspired and has ideas that will give birth to more ideas. The opposite can also happen. Then we won't see a lot of happy faces when the meeting is over. On both occasions, though, we've given energy to others or received it from them. We'll probably keep on thinking about the meeting, whether we're excited or exhausted. Even when we get home, we might go over and over what we should have said and what we might say the next time we're in a similar situation. Wouldn't it be wonderful to be spared all this? To leave work at work and focus on what is important to us when we get home?

To do this, we can use this simple meditation that we call 'Separation'. By 'separation', we mean separating and giving back other people's energies, and also taking back our own energies from others. You may have understood, as we have mentioned it in almost every chapter, that we think it's important to own your own information. If you gain new knowledge but still are stuck in the way your teacher presents it, then you don't have access to your own information, but your teacher's. So you really haven't got very far. It is the same with this book. If you've established communication with your body, your heart, the Earth, the universe and your guardian angel, but interpret everything in the book as we do, well, then you don't have access to your own information, but ours.

It isn't easy to let go of other people's information or energy. In many situations we have been taught to believe that other people know better. Mother and Father know better before we start school. The teachers know better at school. We learn from textbooks. All the theory we learn, we learn from others. And so on.

Sandra held on to other people's energies. Every time she tried to let them go, they returned just as quickly. One day, she had an image of herself as a rubbish skip, collecting the waste of others. At that moment she realized that since early on in her life, she had been taking on others' frustrations and pain, and that she had always had the feeling of being able to carry them better than others.

Sandra was a soother, making people around her feel alright. This was how she felt she was important and valuable to others. She was always there, listening to her friends' problems – which they willingly poured over her. Everybody boasted of how good it was to talk to her. Gradually, though, Sandra had less energy and felt more pain throughout her body. She was actually holding on to other people's energies, because it was through them that she experienced her own value. Perhaps it wasn't that strange that she didn't want to separate from them.

The day Sandra found her own self-worth, however, she managed to let go of everybody else's energies and still trust that people would like her, just because she was worth liking.

There are many reasons why we carry other people's energies. Principally, we do it to cover a weakness in ourselves. Sandra believed that nobody could love her the way she was. Therefore, she came up with creative solutions to get other people's approval. Every time it worked, she got further away from herself, and she carried more and more people in her aura. The 'Separation' meditation helped her to shed light upon this fundamental theme. So, if you can't get the meditation to work at once, try to feel what is blocking it. Only you know the answer, and it is worth a try – being honest with yourself will be rewarding when you go exploring within yourself.

It's also important to separate yourself from those with whom you have private and personal relations. You might know the feeling of being exhausted after a family gathering, even if it was nice. If so, it's very likely that you're carrying some people's energy back from the party in your aura. It is important to separate from spouses and siblings, children and grandchildren, parents and grandparents, aunts and uncles, male friends and female friends – yes, everyone you've been in touch with during the course of the day! You may think that it can't be right to separate yourself from your children or your spouse, or your best friend, for that matter. But it is as hard for your body to carry the energies of the people you like (or feel that you have to like) as it is to carry the energies of those you don't like but are still in your aura. The reason is that it is not your energy but somebody else's. As we mentioned previously, it is only your energy that can nourish your body, just as your blood first and foremost exists for you.

The 'Separation' meditation is very simple but very efficient. It helps you to let other people's stress, rushing and nagging

– yes, other people's energies – remain theirs. It is quick and easy to do, yet powerful. You don't need to focus on people one by one and you can separate yourself from as many as you like at the same time. It is good to do this exercise before going to sleep in the evening, before going home from work or before leaving a party or a dinner. It is hard for people who meet customers, clients, or patients to separate themselves from each and every person, but when you have practised this meditation, you can do it in a few seconds.

☙ **MEDITATION** ☙

SEPARATION

Sit on a chair, close your eyes and take a few deep breaths.

Let your aura click into place.

Put one of your palms, or both, on your heart.

Ask your heart if there is anything it wants to tell you right now.

Contact the Earth and contact the universe from your heart and let the three energies merge in your heart, filling your body and aura with revitalizing energy, the surplus going down your grounding channel. Begin to communicate with your guardian angel from your heart.

Put a magnet outside your aura which attracts everybody else's energies, everybody else's colours that you have borrowed for a while. There might be people there, people you have seen, heard or experienced, or all these things.

If the energies won't go, imagine a switch on the magnet and turn it up to the max.

See, hear, feel or know that the energies are going from you to the magnet. Let your guardian angel take the magnet and just know that the energy will get back where it belongs in a purified form.

Put a new magnet outside your aura that draws your energy back from everybody else.

Let the colours you have lent for a while return to the magnet. (Again: turn the switch of the magnet to the max if the energies won't let go.)

Let your guardian angel give your energy back to you, knowing that it is purified.

Get into communication with your heart again, which is in communication with the heart of the Earth and the heart of the universe, and give to yourself.

Thank yourself, your body and your heart for the steps you've taken.

Thank your guardian angel, the Earth and the universe.

When you have finished, you may open your eyes.

Now we are at the end of our journey. You've encountered yourself in communication with your body (both the physical and the non-physical energy body), your heart, the Earth, the universe and your guardian angel. We hope that you've had some amusing, inspiring, even overwhelming encounters with the true you. Now it is up to you to take charge and use what you've learned to become a master of your own life. You have the chance to take the driver's seat on the road of life, free from being governed by other people's thoughts, patterns and feelings – guided only by your own, in connection with your angels. Let your life approach you from the love within.

We wish you a happy journey.

*A*PPENDIX: TIPS AND ADVICE FOR MEDITATION

For Beginners

A Peaceful Room

It's good if you choose to sit in a special place every time you meditate. Then you'll create a peaceful space where you can get to know yourself. It can be an armchair in the living room, in the bedroom or at the office. You might want to light a candle next to you. Make your place simple and accessible. That way you will develop a routine while you are learning the meditations. Once the meditations are established within you, they are so simple that you can do them anywhere, even on the bus, when you are out shopping or in traffic. If you have any questions about your experiences, please contact us on Facebook (The Spiritual Password) or via Twitter (@spiritualpasswd).

Meditation CD

When we were learning new meditation techniques, we both had to check in books whenever we forgot what the next step was. When that happens, after coming out of meditation you don't experience the continuous joy and depth of feelings a meditation may give. Therefore we created a recording of the meditations in the book – *The Spiritual Password: Meditations* – which is available on CD and to download (please visit www.astarte-inspiration. com for more information). The recorded meditations differ slightly from those in the book, but the message is the same.

Listening to the meditations might be a practical way to proceed, as it avoids trying to remember the different steps by heart or constantly having to look in the book.

Meditating with Other People

It can be an advantage to do the meditations with someone else. It is often difficult to find time and inspiration to sit down to explore yourself through meditation, but two or more people can encourage each other.

It is very likely that you will experience your meditation in a different way from your friend. Be curious about what you find. Explore. Most important: be patient with yourself. We can often recognize patterns in others more easily than in ourselves. And nobody has exactly the same approach: we tackle misfortunes, traumas, joy and success in various ways.

Whatever you feel, be present. Trust that your experience is right for you, no matter what other people experience. This can be a bit difficult if you don't experience anything at all, especially if the person you are with encounters a lot. But it doesn't matter. You're fine the way you are. We're not the same. And that's good.

New Experiences Every Time

The meditation experience often changes from time to time, even if we do the same meditation. The meditations can help us to let go of old resistance or acquired patterns, among other things, and so a change might take place within us which might give rise to a new experience next time. It is like wearing many pairs of spectacles at the same time, with different colours and strengths. Every time we let go of some resistance, it is like taking off one of the pairs. As a result, the world will look slightly different every time. Finally, we will see the world without spectacles, with our own eyes, in our own unique way. That is why how the meditation was last time isn't important. The essential thing is to be in the present and to explore the world from our position right now.

Being Present in the Now

Many people live in the past or the future. 'When I lived there I was happy' is a phrase we often hear people say. Or 'When I move out of this flat/have that car/that job/those clothes/that lover, my life will be perfect.' We plan what we are going to do next week, next month, next year, rushing from one thing to the other without being present in the moment. In fact we miss out on the only time we actually can be present. That is the reason why it is important to practise being in the now. So, allow yourself to let go of what you were doing before the meditation and what you are going to do right afterwards.

Your Encounter with Yourself

It may help to bear in mind that there is no right or wrong way to encounter the Spiritual Password. Remember that everyone has their own unique password and whatever surfaces is of equal value. Some people see images, others see colours or light. Some hear words, others are aware of a feeling. Some people just know, others feel that nothing is happening. Some feel warmth, others cold. Whatever surfaces is of equal value. The most important thing is to dare to encounter yourself with acceptance, honesty and love. Right here and now you have the chance to give yourself a great gift: to throw your inner judge overboard and encounter yourself, including all your shortcomings, with love. Acknowledge that you are fine just the way you are.

By allowing this encounter to take place, you make changes possible through your own power. It is exciting, challenging and often frustrating to encounter yourself. But when you really dare to do it, the rewards are boundless.

Challenges during Meditation

'I Find It Difficult to Concentrate'

This is quite natural. Meditation can be compared with a muscle that needs to be exercised. If you continue, it will solve itself gradually. Maybe you've already found out that it is easier to follow the later meditations than the first ones. If not, just go on, and it will come to you little by little.

'I Fall Asleep during Meditation'

Don't despair – this happens to lots of people. What's happening is that during meditation, the brain frequency is going down. There are different stages of sleep: beta, alpha, theta and delta levels. When you're meditating, you go through all these stages in your brain, just like when you're asleep – only this time you're awake. Your body is not used to being at these levels when you're awake, and that is why it feels as if you're between wakefulness and sleep. On and off, you will even drift in and out of sleep. This will pass as you get into meditation. The information will sink in one way or other. Just trust the process.

'My Body Aches'

Perhaps you think that now you're finally starting to communicate with your body, all the aches and pains that you used to feel should disappear. However, very often they get worse. It is as if your body suddenly understands that it's in contact with you. So it lets you know of all the places that hurt at the same time. It can be compared with a person bottling up their tears. When they finally have a legitimate reason to cry, it all comes out in one go. Maybe that's why some people have an extra good cry at the cinema.

These meditations won't make your body ache more. It is completely safe to meditate. The pains that emerge tend to be those that you have chosen to overlook for some reason or other; perhaps you held them back or didn't listen to them. Maybe that is how you've treated a lot of what your body has tried to communicate to you. But a new era is here. Now you can listen to your body and to your heart. Now your body can unburden itself and point out what is wrong, knowing that you can receive what it has to convey. So the aches will surface from the unconscious to the conscious, but now you have the tools to deal with them. Ask your body what the pains are about. Let go of the blockages, either by breathing them out and taking in more of yourself and your own energy or by using tones. Find the tone of the place where your pain is. Find the tone to letting go. Feel the pain going away. Finally, find the tone of your frequency in the relevant area.

'I Don't Trust my Experience'

If you aren't used to meditating, it can be difficult to trust your experience. How can you know that it's real? Or that it's providing an answer?

The truth is, you can't know. Nobody can prove that what you experienced was an answer from your heart or your guardian angel. Nobody can refute it either. That is why it's great to trust your experiences. We have repeated many times in this book that all information is good. Whatever emerges, it's information about you right now. In an hour, it may be different. But at this very moment, this is the way your body wants to communicate with you. So, instead of dismissing it as bogus or your imagination, try to understand what your body wants to focus on through this experience. Give the communication a chance. When your body understands that you're open to communication, it will gradually become more specific.

The key is to trust yourself. Nobody else in the whole world has your way of encountering yourself, and therefore you cannot compare yourself with others. Their experiences won't be the same either. And you can't try to figure out whether you did it right or wrong, because there is no right or wrong with the encounters during meditation. There are only your experiences when encountering your heart, the heart of the Earth, the heart of the universe and your guardian angel.

'I Don't Experience Anything'

Sometimes when you are meditating, you may find that nothing happens. You see nothing, hear nothing. Everything is black or grey. You may become paralysed or angry because you can't 'make it work'. You start thinking that this meditation stuff is really ridiculous and feel like going and doing something completely different. What can you do about it?

First, are you sure nothing's happening? Maybe you can't see anything, but you can feel something instead. Perhaps there's pressure on your forehead, warmth in your breast, coldness in your legs or pain in your back, head or somewhere else. Encounter whatever emerges.

Secondly, you might be facing resistance to the exercise – you might actually be experiencing something but not allowing yourself to perceive it. So you have to ask yourself what is making you experience this? Is there something you are trying to avoid about yourself? Something you are afraid of rediscovering, perhaps? Something you have promised yourself never to be in touch with again?

Encountering yourself in the way we have described in this book forces you to be honest with yourself. Many people have left honest communication with themselves behind for various reasons. Perhaps they have experienced something painful and not dealt with it. They have to shut off to survive. But then the Spiritual Password on all levels is shut off. If this has happened to you, when you start to open up to the Spiritual Password again, you will find yourself poking into things you have dismissed as non-existent. It can be frightening, provocative, paralysing and strange. This is what we call resistance. You may have resistance to exploring a certain area. You may have resistance to opening up, as there is so much pain there. You may not know *why* the resistance is there. Don't despair. You have already survived the pain. And now you can tackle it from a fresh starting point. What doesn't kill you makes you stronger. So, knowing that you're already stronger, let whatever you are holding back be transformed into something that makes you grow. The way to do this is to shed light on it, to dare to encounter it and to let go of it. That way it will no longer block the Spiritual Password. You might like to do this exercise with someone close, if this makes you feel more secure.

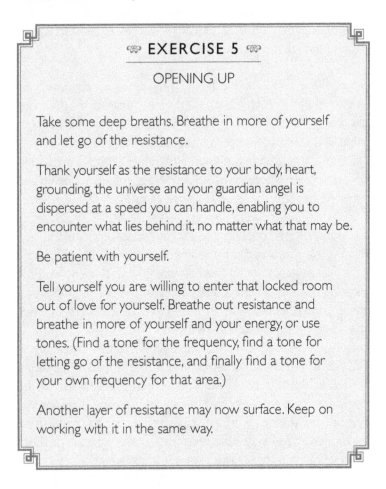

❦ EXERCISE 5 ❦

OPENING UP

Take some deep breaths. Breathe in more of yourself and let go of the resistance.

Thank yourself as the resistance to your body, heart, grounding, the universe and your guardian angel is dispersed at a speed you can handle, enabling you to encounter what lies behind it, no matter what that may be.

Be patient with yourself.

Tell yourself you are willing to enter that locked room out of love for yourself. Breathe out resistance and breathe in more of yourself and your energy, or use tones. (Find a tone for the frequency, find a tone for letting go of the resistance, and finally find a tone for your own frequency for that area.)

Another layer of resistance may now surface. Keep on working with it in the same way.

When you feel that you have done enough for the day, you can meditate again to see if anything has changed or not. Good luck!

'I Can't Seem to Get Any Answers'

We're used to being guided by common sense, to predetermining our experiences and letting reason rule. When we meditate, however, we begin to open to our unconscious. So, the fact that you're not getting answers to your questions during meditation is great. It simply means that you've started to open to the unconscious and the Spiritual Password. It may well be that you will get the answers in time – they'll just come in a different way than expected. Keep on listening to yourself, uncritically and with acceptance.

'I Can't Feel my Heartbeat in my Body'

Everyone has different ways of communicating with themselves. Some can feel their heartbeat everywhere in their body, others can only to a lesser extent, maybe only in their chest, or even not at all. Well, it doesn't matter what other people do – what's important is how you feel your heartbeat. Explore where you can feel it. Does that change from day to day? Is your heartbeat always absent from a particular place or is it perceptible from time to time? Explore. Play with your experience. Have fun getting to know yourself in this way.

Overlooking or Underestimating our Experiences

Even if we have miracles under our very nose, it's surprising how often we manage to overlook them. We meet our experiences with the ego structure within – for example, by adopting the victim's role, just like a four-year-old whose need wasn't satisfied, or out of fear of being condemned as worthless. Our ego structure developed in response to our past experiences. But now things are different. We can allow ourselves to receive exactly what we need, based on the person we are today. We can allow ourselves to encounter the experiences the Spiritual Password will bring with respect, acceptance and love for ourselves.

$\mathscr{A}$CKNOWLEDGEMENTS

We would like to thank our children, who teach us more about life every day.

We would like to thank Ari for continuous support and encouragement.

We would like to thank our parents, who provided us with the starting point to become who we are today.

We would like to thank our students, who loyally turn up for classes and make our dream come true every day. Without them, this book would not exist.

Thanks to all those who unreservedly contributed with their personal stories.

Words cannot describe the appreciation we feel for Carina Scheele Carlsen's many contributions to enabling this book to see the light of day.

Thanks to Hay House Publishing UK for believing in us enough to take us on board, rocketing this book to the next level.

Thank you to the design team at Hay House UK for the divine physical details.

Thanks also to Lizzie Hutchins for eminent editorial effort and for your keen eye for detail.

Thanks to Lena Kristiansson Torp and Ann Cathrin Torp in Strong Design for beautiful pictures explaining the aura.

Thanks to Mona Nordøy and her crew for wonderful photos. Thanks to Marthe Kveli Valeberg for making us look divine.

Thanks to Camilla Jensen for her wonderful recipes from the book *Bønner og Linser* (Beans and Lentils).

Thanks to Victoria Rikede for acknowledging our work and translating this book into English.

Thanks to everyone opening doors for us in regard to this book and our work, enabling more people to connect with their Spiritual Password and their angels.

Thanks to Ida Berntsen for the editorial work on *Meet Your Guardian Angel*, the Norwegian version of this book, upon which this book is based.

Thanks to all the people who have taught us something along the way. You have all been our teachers, though we did not always realize it at the time.

Thanks to our guardian angels for encouragement and for light nudges when we have hesitated.

Finally, thanks to ourselves for the steps we have taken in this process.

$\mathscr{B}$IBLIOGRAPHY

Angelo, Jack. *Your Healing Power: A Comprehensive Guide to Channeling Your Healing Energies*. London: Judy Piatkus Ltd, 1994

Astell, Christine. *Discovering Angels: Wisdom, Healing, Destiny*. London: Duncan Baird Publishers Ltd., 2005

Atwater, P. M. H. *Beyond the Indigo Children: The New Children and the Coming of the Fifth World*. Vermont: Bear & Company, 2005

Bjerke, André. *Collected Poems: 1940–1953*. Oslo: Aschehoug & Co., 1977

Bøhle, Solveig. *When the Body Remembers What You Would Like to Forget*. Oslo: Bazar Forlag, 2008

Brown, Simon G. *Chi Energy Workbook: A Practical Guide to the Essence That Links All Holistic Therapies*. New Delhi: Sterling, 2003

Bye, Erik, and Krogvold, Morten. *I Am Here! Are You There?: A Story of the Art of Communication.* Oslo: Telenor, 1997

Choquette, Sonia. *Ask Your Guides: Connecting to Your Divine Support System.* Carlsbad: Hay House, Inc., 2006

Cortens, Theolyn. *Working with Your Guardian Angel: An Inspirational 12-week Programme for Finding Your Life's Purpose.* London: Piatkus Books Ltd, 2006

Working with Archangels: Your Path to Transformation and Power. London: Piatkus Books Ltd, 2007

Emoto, Masaru. *The Hidden Messages in Water.* Hillsboro: Beyond Words Publishing, Inc., 2004

The Miracle of Water. Hillsboro: Beyond Words Publishing, Inc., 2007

Jensen, Camilla. *Beans and Lentils.* Oslo: Gyldendal, 2009

Johansson, Lena. *Reiki: A Key to Your Personal Healing Power.* Wisconsin: Lotus Press, 2001

Kelder, Peter. *Ancient Secret of the Fountain of Youth.* Gig Harbor: Harbor Press, Inc., 1985

Lagerlöf, Selma, et al. *The Angel by the Apal Crescent.* Oslo: Verbum Forlag, 2006

Lipton, Bruce H. *The Biology of Belief: Unleashing the Power of Consciousness, Matter and Miracles.* Carlsbad: Hay House, Inc., 2005

Spontaneous Evolution: Our Positive Future and a Way to Get There from Here. Carlsbad: Hay House, Inc., 2011

Mayes, Sherron. *Be Your Own Psychic: Tapping the Innate Power Within.* Berkeley: Ulysses Press, 2004

McTaggart, Lynn. *The Field: The Quest for the Secret Force of the Universe.* London: HarperCollinsPublishers, 2001

Mercier, Patricia. *Chakras: Balance Your Energy Flow for Health and Harmony.* London: Godsfield Press Ltd, 2000

Pearl, Dr Eric. *The Reconnection: Heal Others, Heal Yourself.* Carlsbad: Hay House, Inc., 2001

Sennov, Anni. *Crystal Children, Indigo Children and Adults of the Future.* Greve Strand: Good Adventures Publishing, 2004

The Three Initiates. *The Kybalion: A Study of the Hermetic Philosophy of Ancient Egypt and Greece.* Chicago: The Yogi Publication Society, 1912

Tjalve, Eskild, and Birgit. *Når ånd og stof modes: Den Ny Tids Verdensbillede* (Not translated). Bogans Forlag, 1998

Vander, Arthur J., Sherman, James H., Luciano, Dorothy S. *Human Physiology: The Mechanisms of Body Function.* New York: McGraw-Hill, 1990

Virtue, Doreen. *Angel Medicine: How to Heal the Body and Mind with the Help of the Angels.* Carlsbad: Hay House, Inc., 2005

Divine Magic: The Seven Sacred Secrets of Manifestation. Carlsbad: Hay House, 2006

Wergeland, Henrik. 'Evening Prayer' from *Den store dikt og regleboka.* Oslo: Aschehoug, 2004

Williamson, Marianne. *A Return to Love: Reflections on the Principles of "A Course in Miracles".* New York: HarperCollins Publishers, Inc., 1993

ABOUT THE AUTHORS

Photographer: Mona Nordøy

Princess Märtha Louise was born into the Norwegian royal family. Being in the public eye for so many years has been both challenging and educational. In addition to her official duties, Princess Märtha Louise has been a clairvoyant all her life, and studied to become a physiotherapist and a Rosen Method Practitioner. She has written books for children, hosted a number of TV shows and was a member of the Norwegian National Showjumping Team. Princess Märtha Louise lives in London with her husband, their three children and their dog.

Elisabeth Nordeng has studied energy work for several years and, in addition to being a clairvoyant, has had a close connection to the angels since early childhood. Growing up she had a great spiritual longing, which resulted in an awakening of consciousness in her early twenties. For many years she chose to do the most important work of all: being a full-time mother. Yet a longing for answers to many questions about spirituality led her to a course in energy readings during which she met Princess Märtha Louise. Elisabeth lives in Oslo with her four children and two dogs.

Together, Princess Märtha Louise and Elisabeth run Astarte Inspiration, which they founded 2007 to offer courses in self-development with a spiritual dimension. They work with innovative spiritual tools for the new era, specializing in the angelic realm, and tour the world giving inspirational talks and workshops.

 @spiritualpasswd

 The Spiritual Password

www.astarte-inspiration.com

CPSIA information can be obtained
at www.ICGtesting.com
Printed in the USA
LVHW090154190420
654024LV00001B/103

9 781781 802670